# BEAR MARKET GAME PLAN

---

## Strategies for Investing
in a Volatile Market

# BEAR MARKET GAME PLAN

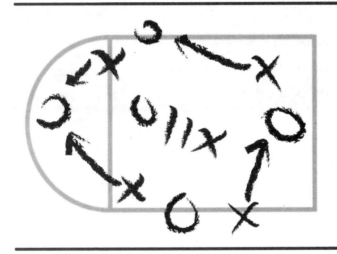

## Strategies for Investing in a Volatile Market

Ross Jardine

*Bear Market Game Plan, Strategies for Investing in a Volatile Market* is designed to provide accurate and authoritative information regarding investing in the stock market. It is understood that the publisher nor the author is not engaged in rendering legal, accounting, or other professional service. If legal advice or other expert assistance is required, the services of a competent professional person should be sought.

Managing Editor: Ross Jardine
Editor: Julilyn Haacke Wells
Cover Design: Cory Lorenzen
Interior Design: Julilyn Haacke Wells

# Table of Contents

The year 2000 was a very memorable year, especially in the stock market. Everyone seemed convinced the millennium bug would crash computers all over the world. Turns out it was the stock market that the bug infected.

In the second half of 2000, the market turned bearish and many investors saw much of the gains they'd made over the past few years wiped out in a matter of months. This was easily one of the most volatile periods in the history of the stock market.

The explosive growth of the Internet and a raging bull market has brought millions of new investors into the market over the past decade. Many investors grew accustomed to 20+ percent returns and lost sight of the fact that markets don't always go up. In fact, many investors borrowed heavily and poured every last cent into the market figuring the almost certain windfall would easily cover the interest.

In the basic investing seminars my company teaches all over the world, we expose investors to things like technical analysis and fundamental analysis. Investors learn how to read charts and understand some of the most common technical indicators. We also introduce people to some basic strategies, like using covered calls to generate income and playing stock splits with options.

Over the past decade, most investors have had a decidedly bullish bias, and rightly so. Now that the market has changed so dramatically, many investors are struggling with the fact that what has worked so well for them during the past decade simply isn't working anymore. Unwilling to admit things have changed, they continue to apply their bullish strategies only to find themselves digging an even deeper financial hole. Many have become so afraid of losing more money, they simply pull out of the market completely.

Markets never go up forever, and investors need to learn to recognize the major market trends and adjust their strategies accordingly. The natural tendency of most investors is to have a bullish bias, which is the single biggest weakness when the market turns bearish.

Now we find ourselves in a much more challenging circumstance: the markets are as volatile as they have ever been with a bias towards the downside. Judging by the emails and from feedback we get from the tens of thousands of students who have come through our courses from all around the world, we feel a great need to help you through this very difficult circumstance.

This is one of the reasons I put together this book, calling it *Bear Market Game Plan, Strategies for Investing in a Volatile Market*, as that is exactly what many investors need to weather the storm ... a simple plan. My intent is not to scare people with use of the words "bear market." This book is simply to introduce you to some strategies for surviving and even profiting in a very volatile market. I'm confident it will give you some of the tools and resources you need to restore your confidence in investing in the markets and to get back in control of your portfolio.

Many of you will notice that some of the things I address in this book are just slight variations of the strategies you would use during a bull market. My intent is to teach you how to succeed in this very challenging market right now. Or, at the very least, to teach you how to protect yourself against catastrophic losses and help you preserve your capital.

Historically, bear markets don't last too long, but those who have lived through one will tell you the memory they leave lasts forever. People never look at investing in the stock market with the same level of confidence ever again. But once the bear market ends, you can again start applying some of the more bullish strategies and approaches you have been taught or have used in the past.

The purpose of this book is to give you a few simple steps you can take to preserve your capital, or perhaps find some opportunity where most investors see none. The motivation for this book comes from the thousands of emails my company get from our students. These are investors just like you who want to know what steps they can take to protect their portfolios from falling stock prices.

In this book I am going to help you understand exactly how to survive in a downtrending market, and perhaps even find opportunities and profits ... if you're willing to apply some simple bearish strategies.

First of all, let's take a look at the overall big picture of the market right now—at the time of printing—and get a feel for where we are at and what has happened.

So what is a *bear market* anyway? Probably everyone has heard the term, but by definition, what does it really mean? We associate bear markets with falling stock prices. If we look at the last seven months of the year 2000, we can see that some very dramatic things took place in the market ... particularly the NASDAQ market (and for those of us who have enjoyed the great boom in technology stocks over the last few years, it hurts!). While every sector of the market has been affected, technology stocks, the Internet stocks in particular, have been the hardest hit.

By pulling up some of the numbers on the market, you can get a better idea of just how bad it has been. Most experts will typically define a bear market as any decline in the major market index of 20 percent or more. Looking again at the last seven months of the year 2000, we saw a near 50 percent decline in the NASDAQ market from the March highs. Many of the technology stocks that led us through the great bull market of the last seven years are now trading at just a fraction of their value from just seven months earlier.

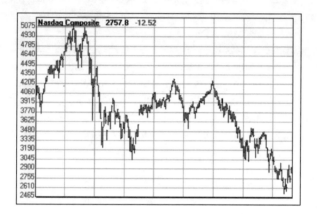

The month of November 2000 was one of the most volatile months in the history of the stock market, with the exception of a couple of bad months in 1987 and 1997.

Taking a look at some of the other major indexes, you can kind of get a feel for what happened. The Dow Jones Industrial Average is down about 10 percent over the same period, a mere correction by normal standards.

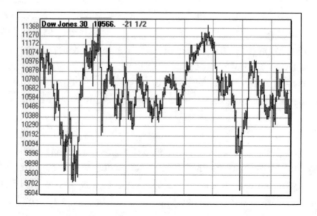

The S&P 500, which is made up of a much broader group of

stocks, is down about 16 percent. Obviously a lot of those fallen technology stocks have had a bearing on this index, as well.

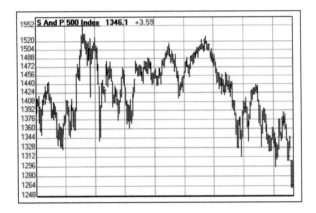

It's easy to see by looking at any of these graphs that the markets are falling. The fact you are reading this book would indicate that you, like many other investors, are feeling a little frustrated. You're angry ... you're upset ... and you're disappointed. And above it all, you're poorer than you were just a few months ago.

Nobody likes losing money. It's one of my least favorite things. Unfortunately, over the last several months of 2000, many investors experienced significant losses. Most didn't see the bear market coming and thus didn't take the proper steps to prepare their portfolio for it.

I want you to step back for a moment away from the emotions of things not having gone the way you had hoped they would. Try to see what you could have done differently to minimize the impact of the bear market on your portfolio.

We're going to look at how we can approach this new set of circumstances to find opportunities, or at the very least protect ourselves and preserve our capital. Your goal should be to prepare yourself for any market conditions you may encounter. You need to create a personal plan that fits your objectives, your tolerance for risk, and your lifestyle.

While the content of this book specifically addresses investing in a bear market, I'm certain you'll find the information equally helpful in keeping you focused in the next bull market that will almost certainly follow. Let's introduce you to the topics we will address.

### Emotions

First we will focus on the emotions of investing. A lot of people say that the bulk of investing is not what you do in the market or with your broker, but what takes place between your ears. (And I think that sometimes it takes place in your heart or in your gut, as well.) The biggest battle most investors wage is with their emotions; it's a lifelong battle.

In my experience, I've noticed that the best investors tend to be almost mechanical in their approach to investing. While one can never totally eliminate emotions from investing decisions, successful investors are able to minimize their impact.

### Trends

We also want to take a look at trends. I think it is important to really understand trends. In the chapter on trends, I will give you some very specific things to help you identify trends, to be more aware of them, and to make them become a basic element of your stock research and investment decisions. This is important because it is going to help keep you out of trouble and help you stay on the right side of the market. I think you will find that this simple concept will help you choose the best strategies to employ when market conditions change. Identifying and following the correct trends can also help you protect yourself from declines in the market that could reduce your capital and limit your ability to recover after you have sustained some losses.

### Stop Loss Order

We're going to remind you of one of the most simple tools for protecting yourself against sudden declines in the market: stop loss orders. Most of you have heard of them or even used them from time to time. My goal is to show you exactly how and when to use them. One of the problems many people have when they have sustained some substantial losses is that they think it is too late to do anything about it. In most cases it is not too late. I think you need to incorporate stops into your investment program.

The time to decide to use a stop is not when the market has begun to fall, but when you're considering entering a new position. Stops are one of the easiest ways to preserve your capital while keeping you out of situations in which emotions can take over and make any decision very difficult to make.

When the markets turn and the situations change, we need to come back to the basics, "stops" being one of them. I like them because they help protect us from sudden declines in the market that we're probably not anticipating.

### *Finding Opportunity in a Down Market*

The second part of this book addresses finding opportunity in a down market. There is plenty of opportunity in a bear market for those who wish to apply bearish strategies.

There are two approaches we're going to address: one using put options and the other shorting stock. We will take a good look at put options. This is a strategy most investors don't understand ... and when people don't understand something, they tend to avoid it. Now is a great time for you to learn how to recognize opportunities for trading puts. My goal is to help you completely understand the basic skills needed to become a confident put player.

In addition to being a put player, there is another approach you can take that doesn't involve options. It is called shorting stock. Although many of you have heard of the term, I am going to define it and discuss its pros along with its cons. However, I consider the strategy of selling short to be a lot more aggressive than that of buying puts, which means my focus will be more towards the put plays than short selling.

Most investors are not well suited for short selling because of all of the additional risk involved. With option plays, we are able to

limit our risk and keep it to a very specific amount. We are looking at put options in two different ways: first by using them to
profit from declines in the market, and second by using them as
insurance policies to protect the stock positions we still have in
our accounts. Both of these are very valid ways to use put
options, and we want to cover both of them so that you can have
the confidence to incorporate them into your individual portfolio.

### *Collar*

The final thing we want to talk about in this book is a strategy
that is used in sideways or downtrending markets. It is called a
collar. This is a strategy that has been around for a long time. It
is one of the most simple and conservative option strategies there
is. A collar is basically a way for you to structure an option trade
so that you get free insurance against a decline in a stock you
own.

We talk about puts as having value in terms of protecting ourselves against falls in the market or falls in an individual stock,
but I will show you a simple way to actually generate, from your
investments, all the money it takes to buy these insurance policies. Just remember, it's called a collar and I'm sure you will not
only enjoy learning about it. You will probably ask yourself,
"Why hasn't anybody ever told me about this before now?"

# Chapter One

# Emotions of Investing in a Bear Market

Now, let's just step back, take a deep breath, and look at the over-all market. I want you to make an assessment of the emotions you are feeling along with the things that you see in the market. Now let's see how these emotions are having an impact on what you are doing with your money.

Without question, the biggest challenge most investors face is controlling their emotions. Everyone has a point where they cross over the line of reason and logic and allow their emotions to take over. If we could somehow identify where that point is, we could become better at avoiding it.

The point where you cross over that line is not something you can figure out in your head. We know when we have crossed the line because we feel it in the pit of our stomach. I know you know *that* feeling I'm talking about.

It's when you wake up at 3:00 a.m. and turn on the television to CNBC to check the S&P futures to see if you can get a read on whether the market will open up or down that day. It's when you're out with your family and all you can think about is how you're going to break the news to your spouse that you lost the bulk of your children's college funds.

We all know the feeling of being in a situation where there appears to be no way out—so we do the natural thing and panic.

Only after making a hasty decision do we finally realize that we usually buy or sell at the worst possible time. Emotions cloud your judgment ... and if ever you need a clear head, it's when you're making a decision about your money.

It is very important that you understand there are many different emotions involved in investing. At opposite ends of the spectrum of the emotions that we feel as investors are fear and greed. In a bull market it's our overwhelming sense of greed that drives most of our investment decisions. We become confident ... we think everything is going up. We have become part of the crowd and are simply buying because everyone else is ... and everyone seems to be making money no matter what he/she buys.

In a bear market, fear takes over. We're controlled by our fear. I think fear is a far more powerful emotion than greed for most investors. While greed gets us into the market when opportunity may be minimal, fear will keep us out of the market when opportunity is plentiful. Greed creates losses and creates lost opportunity. These emotional extremes are usually a signal that the market has hit either a top or bottom.

Fear is the emotion I want to focus on in this chapter. Most of us are afraid of losing money, and if you're not, you probably should be. The fear of losing money can be paralyzing. I talk to many people who have bought a stock and have held on to it for a long period of time. They are classic buy-and-hold investors, and they have convinced themselves that they can ride out any downturn in the market.

There is nothing wrong with investing for the long haul, but, unfortunately many of those investments are now down 10, 20, 30, and 40 ... some down 90 percent. If you're still holding one of those e-commerce stocks that were all the rage in 1999, you know the feeling. This bear market didn't stop with just the weak companies. Even the market leaders like Cisco, Intel, Dell, and Microsoft are now trading for significantly less than they were at the beginning of 2000.

Most investors in this position have known all along that they should have gotten out of these stocks long before now. There were plenty of signs and signals along the way to alert them that the market was changing.

In Spencer Johnson's book, *Who Moved My Cheese?*, the main characters search through a maze that symbolizes life to find cheese that is symbolic for happiness, money, and success. They search hard and finally find the cheese. Each day they return to enjoy the cheese. Life is good.

Then, one day, there is no more cheese. But it wasn't a sudden event. Each day the supply of cheese was less and less. Some of the characters recognized this trend and began to prepare a new search in the maze for more cheese. The other characters didn't recognize these changes and found themselves in a state of shock when the cheese finally disappeared.

While the one group immediately took off into the maze and eventually found a new supply of cheese, the other group sat around wondering who moved the cheese and hoped it would magically show up again. It never did and they, too, eventually had to enter the maze and begin to search for more cheese.

Compare the cheese to stocks ... stocks people own that drop in value. They fail to see the changes that happen along the way and then they act surprised when their stocks are no longer doing well. They wonder who moved the cheese.

Had they been more aware of the changing trends in the market, they could have better prepared themselves for the drop. They could have taken precautionary measures to protect their investments from loss.

Too many investors fall in love with their stocks and lose sight of the fact that they own stocks to make money. When the opportunity to make money is gone, they need to look to a new stock for a better opportunity.

Changing trends are a lot like a train traveling across the country. Let's call this the losing train. It doesn't just go from point A to point B; it makes lots of stops along the way. Each time the losing train stops, the conductor asks the passengers if they want to get off. Most choose to stay on. When the train finally gets to point B, the passengers are wondering how they could have stayed on it for so long when there were so many opportunities to get off when the train was clearly not headed in the direction they intended to go.

The paralyzing nature of fear causes us to avoid making hard decisions. This delay usually ends up compounding an already bad situation. We hold on to a stock for so long that we finally decide it's too late to do anything. We continue to hold our investment, like a lottery ticket, hoping there will be some miraculous recovery. The recovery rarely comes. These trades are the ones that usually result in those catastrophic losses.

As I travel the country talking to investors, I often ask how many of them could have done better last year on their overall portfolio by two or three percent had they simply eliminated one or two bad investments. It's amazing to see an entire room full of investors nod their heads in the affirmative. One of the easiest ways to build a portfolio is to avoid the catastrophic losses we so often seem to create.

It is amazing that the majority of these people say they knew they should have gotten out but didn't. Most of them were caught up in the paralysis of fear or had a lack of confidence in their own ability to read a chart and make a decision. This kept them in the investment far longer than they had ever intended.

Let's take a look at why someone—if they knew the stock was going to decline 30, 40, 50, or 60 percent—would stay in it for more than a 10 to 15 percent decline. Is it in hopes of the stock bouncing back? In order to analyze this, we need to look at the individual aspects of fear and break them down.

The first thing to look at is that we all have a fear of losing money. Nobody likes to lose money. Often times our emotions make us stay in something, even though we know that it may not be the best place to be. Sometimes we just can't come to grips with recognizing that we have lost money. This is what I refer to as the paralysis of fear; it keeps us in a position longer than we should be in it.

The next thing, which I am sure many of you have experienced over the last couple years with the market going up, is the fear of giving back a profit. Now ask yourself, have you ever been in a position where a stock went in your favor and created a profit for you, but then you were so afraid of giving that profit back that you sold too soon? Then when the stock continued to run a long way beyond that, you were on the sidelines kicking yourself for getting out so soon. Fear also kept you from getting back in because you convinced yourself that the investment would drop the minute you did.

It was the fear you had of giving back the profit that caused you to make an emotional decision to get out too early. Maybe there wasn't any real reason or any signal on the indicators or graphs, or anything on the news you were following that said, "Get out now." But your simple fear of not giving back your profit caused you to do it.

Giving back a paper profit is a lot like having a stranger reach into your pocket and help themselves to a few dollars from your billfold. You feel violated or robbed. It's the fear of this situation that motivates many investors to cash out of great investments long before the full benefit of their wise decision is realized. We've all heard the saying: "Let your profits ride and cut your losses short." For many investors it is just the opposite: "Let your losses run and cut your profits short."

Selling too soon is better than selling too late, but I'll discuss that later. We also recognize that when we get into a trade that is working out, we want to stay in it as long as we can. So now we know that the fear of giving back our profits is something that often leads to an emotional decision to get out too early.

The last thing is admitting we are wrong. It is not fun to have to admit that we've made a mistake. But you need to realize that not being honest with yourself will usually just compound the problem. You shouldn't take these things so personal.

The fact is, you can do everything right, you can do everything you've been taught and everything you have learned on your own ... and you can still lose money. You can apply everything you know about investing, and you are still not guaranteed success, even if you do it perfectly right.

There are always things that surprise us ... things that change the picture. It's how you adapt to the change that will determine whether change becomes a roadblock or a speed bump on the way to accomplishing your investment objectives. The sign of a really disciplined investor is one who can quickly admit a mistake or that the markets moved against him/her and take a small loss and move on. Many investors take losses personally; they say they've made a mistake. We think that if we sell, our spouse or broker is going to find out about it and be disappointed.

We equate a loss with admitting we made a mistake. Oftentimes it's that fear of admitting a mistake or the fear of admitting a loss that keeps us in a trade too long. It does not mean that you have made a mistake, and you don't need to take it that way. Losses are as much a part of investing as profits. It's how you deal with them that determines your long-term success or failure.

At first a loss is just a number on the statement your broker sends you each month; but when it is no longer just on paper, you have to be able to admit that you had a loss and move on. Unfortunately, for a lot of people this is a challenge. We all need to learn to deal with losses and overcome those negative thoughts.

I think it is important for you to understand that you do not have control over the stock market; you don't have control over an individual stock or option. You don't control the mutual funds or any of the other investment vehicles you choose to invest in. You simply need to be able to monitor their movements using the best available resources and information, and make decisions that will hopefully keep you on the right side of things.

There is one other fear I want to point out to you that is a little more subtle. It is the fear of being an eternal optimist. I don't think there is any doubt that most people who invest in the market do so because they want to buy something and see it go higher.

I got my first securities license in 1987. Some of you will remember that year as one of the most volatile in the history of the market. That was the year we had the "Bloody Monday" in the stock market when the Dow fell over 500 points in a single day. I think you'd agree that starting out in the financial services industry in this type of environment would be a real challenge. I noticed quickly that the investment strategies producing profits when the market was falling were the ones that were working the best. I wondered why more of the brokers in the office weren't selling these investments to their clients.

One day I stopped into the sales manager's office to discuss this idea I had. I thought I could increase my production by changing from selling bullish investments to selling bearish investments. This seasoned manager put his arm around me and said he agreed with my assessment of the market and was even doing some of these things in his personal account with his own money.

He then went on to tell me that people want to buy things that will go up in value. He said it was the "American way." He also told me that the minute I stop selling dreams, I wouldn't be able to sell a thing. It didn't make any sense to me. All the other brokers continued to encourage their clients to buy more and average down. I chose to leave the industry and just focus on my own account.

There is a powerful motivation to be invested in the market all the time. The problem is that we often ignore the signals that are in front of us and continue to do the things we've always been doing or apply bullish strategies, even though the market is clearly bearish. We keep trying to pick the bottoms, and the bottoms keep dropping out.

When you find yourself hoping, wishing, and praying for things to get better, that's a sure sign you've fallen prey to your emotions.

The eternal optimist is one who ignores changing trends and continues to apply bullish strategies in bearish markets. If you're not willing to adjust your approach when the market trends change, you need to at least recognize the change and move to the sidelines and wait it out. Those who can't overcome their bullish tendencies could lose it all before the market turns positive again.

You need to recognize the signals and get out of the market and stay on the sidelines until the market again conforms to your strategies. Some of you need to look back and ask yourself, "Over the last year, would I have been better off sitting with my money in cash and earning interest on it, even if it was just in a money market account making 4 to 5 percent a year?"

Would that have produced a better return than what you made in the stock market over the same period? Some of you may, unfortunately, have to say yes. So that's the challenge. And, we are not admitting defeat by moving our money out of stocks and putting them in more conservative investments like bonds or interest bearing money market accounts. This is something people have to overcome. We have been spoiled with the 20 percent or better returns in the market over the past few years, and now we've got to become willing to go against the trend and risk huge losses and accept that the market has changed and be content with a more conservative rate of return on our money.

Any return is better than a loss, in my book. I want to focus my investments where there is the best opportunity to grow my account and avoid losses. If that's in a money market account, so be it.

Let's recap the key points of managing our emotions:

## The Emotions of Investing

◆ Fear
- Of losing money
- Of giving back a profit
- Of admitting you're wrong

◆ Eternal Optimism
- Fighting the trend

The more you are able to control your emotions and limit their impact on your investment decisions, the better investor you will become.

# Chapter Two

# The Trend Is Your Friend

A number of years ago I accompanied a group of Boy Scouts on a river rafting trip to the beautiful Salmon River in Idaho. Our guide was a veteran of hundreds of trips down the river in rafts, riverboats, and canoes. He knew every little nook and cranny along the way.

The night before our journey down the river began, our guide talked to us at length around the campfire about the many things that could go wrong in order to help us prepare for the challenges that lie ahead. However, the Scouts were more interested in roasting their hot dogs and marshmallows than listening to this wise guide.

He talked about the power of a river as it moves through the canyons. He mentioned dozens of times that it's impossible to fight the current. He told us that if we tipped over and found ourselves in the water, we should not try to swim against the current, but keep our feet forward and be on the lookout for oncoming objects to keep from crashing into them. He said that to get out of the current, you must swim with it and work your way to safety on the banks.

We enjoyed two days of running the river without any incident. It was great fun for everyone. After going through increasingly difficult rapids without any trouble, our confidence in our ability was high. We began taking bigger and bigger risks, much to the dismay of our overly cautious guide.

All that changed when the raft I was guiding got caught in a hole in one of the largest rapids and shot straight up in the air like a rocket, sending the six boys in the front of the raft crashing down on me in the back and plunging all of us into the icy, churning waters.

Our cocky confidence immediately turned to terror as each of us struggled to keep our heads above the water and swim towards the upside-down raft. Two of the boys and myself were unable to reach the raft before being swept downstream in the swift-moving current.

I consider myself a strong swimmer, but even with the help of a life jacket it was difficult to stay above the thrashing current. One of the boys was able to reach a calm spot in the rapids and swim to the bank, but the other boy and myself were still stuck in the middle of the river and were unable to get out of the current. No matter how hard I tried, I could not catch up to the young boy who was now over 100 feet ahead of me. He was terrified ... and it was the most helpless feeling I've ever had not to be able to reach him to help him get out of the current.

About this time, one of the other leaders raced past us in a truck on the shore and threw a line across a narrow stretch of the river a few hundred yards in front of the young Scout to give him something to grab as he floated past. Seeing that the boy was going to be rescued, I made one last effort to swim to shore. Expending all the energy I could muster, I eventually was able to break the bond of the current and swim into some calm water near the bank. It wasn't until I was in water that was barely a foot deep that I was able to stand up. I had tried several times, but was instantly knocked down by the swift current.

I learned a valuable less from this terrifying experience: it's almost impossible to fight the current. The power of the current is deceptively strong. It was only when I swam with the current that I was able to make any progress to the shore. No amount of effort could keep me from being pulled along by the strong current.

In many respects, the stock market is also like the river. There is a current that flows, constantly pulling individual stocks up and down with it. It's a subtle thing at times, and like raging rapids at others. The key to survival for investors in the market is to recognize the current, respect its power, and apply strategies that benefit from the direction of the flow.

In the market the current is called the trend. You may not realize it, but the trend is as powerful as any current or tide you'll find in the water. Fighting the trend is as difficult as trying to swim upstream in the Salmon River. You may be able to hold your ground for a minute or two, but eventually the trend will win and sweep you away with it.

When I went through training as a new broker, I heard the saying "the trend is your friend" at least a hundred times. I thought I knew what it meant, but it wasn't until I had lost tens of thousands of my own hard-earned money that I really understood what it meant to make the trend your friend.

I think this is one of the most fundamental aspects of investing in the stock market and I want to take a few minutes to make sure you understand how to recognize trends and choose a strategy that will work in the current market conditions.

Each day before I go looking for new investments, I make a quick check of the major trends in the overall market, the leading sectors, and the stocks I'm following or invested in. Before I put any money at risk, I want to know which direction the current is moving so I can find the best stocks and apply the appropriate strategy.

If I determine the trend is not favorable, it's easy to turn off the computer and head to the golf course. My experience in the river and my many mistakes with my own investments have taught me that fighting the trend is almost always a losing battle. I consider a day on the golf course a whole lot more fun than losing money in the market.

In my seminars, I tell my students that finding a great stock in a bear market can be a bit like finding a needle in a haystack. It's hard work. In a bull market, great stocks are plentiful and much easier to find. Just look at all the new investors who made huge profits by following the crowd and buying Internet stocks in 1999. They may not have any idea what they were doing, but it seemed like every stock was going up and the only way to lose was to not buy anything. It was like looking for a needle in a whole haystack of needles.

It was hard to lose and confidence was high—just like after two days of running the river. Then, in March of 2000, the raft tipped over and those investors found themselves floating in the icy current unable to swim to shore. They kept buying the same stocks hoping things would change, but this only compounded their losses and frustration.

For those who failed to change their approach and adapt to the new trend in the market, they most likely ended up wiping out several years of profits in just a few short months. Only those who changed their strategy to one that worked in the new market conditions could begin to take back control of their portfolio. The river and the market have many similarities. Failing to recognize changing trends can result in a financial drowning.

So how can you spot the trends in the market and adjust your approach to make sure it's following the trend? I think the easiest way is to use charts and simple moving averages to identify trends and recognize when they change.

As I mentioned earlier, I like to identify three specific trends before I go looking for new investments.

## The Trend Is Your Friend

♦ Know the trend
   ◆ Market
   ◆ Sector
   ◆ Stock

♦ Don't fight the trend

Once you recognize the trend, it's important not to fight it, but invest with it.

I like to use moving averages to spot trends in the market, sectors, and stocks. This method is fast and easy once you know what you're looking for and it will keep you out of a lot of trouble if you use this tool to help you decide where and how you invest your money.

There are three possible trends you can see:

1. Up
2. Down
3. Sideways

If the trend is not clear to you, the best advice is to sit out until you see it clearly. My motto is, "When in doubt, sit out."

Depending on whether you're a long or short-term investor, you may need to change the moving average you use to help you identify the trend. Short-term investors—those who don't mind moving in and out of investments every few weeks or months—may use a 30-day moving average to identify trends that help them make their decisions.

Longer-term investors, the buy-and-hold crowd, should use longer moving averages, like a 200-day moving average. The shorter the moving average, the more sensitive it is to changes in the market. These changes could provide you with entry and exit signals on your individual investments.

Longer-term investors are not worried about moving in and out on every swing in the market, but want to stay invested as long as the major long-term trend stays in tact. By using a longer-term moving average, the trend changes will be fewer and far between. The longer moving average will smooth out the ups and downs in the market or stock and give fewer buy-and-sell signals. So the first thing you need to do is pick a moving average that fits your approach and objectives.

Here's an example. This is a one-year graph of Intel (INTC) with a 30-day moving average plotted on it. The moving average is the smooth solid line that follows the daily movements of the stock. Notice how it smoothes out the jagged movement of the stock.

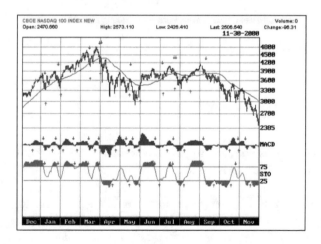

Let's follow the moving average from the left to the right of the chart and see if we can't determine the trend of Intel. At the far left side of the graph you can see the stock is dramatically moving up and the moving average is pointing straight upward. This is clearly an uptrend. Around the end of March, INTC crosses the

30-day moving average and begins to roll over and point down. This is the start of a short downtrend that lasts for about two months before the stock once again crosses the moving average, this time moving up through it.

The stock then moves sideways for about three months. Notice how the moving average line flattens out while the stock is moving sideways. The stock breaks down in September and the moving average quickly follows. The stock is now in a pronounced downtrend and the moving average is acting like a ceiling. The stock makes several attempts to cross the moving average, but each time it hits this area of resistance and bounces down.

Let's look at the same stock with a longer-term moving average to see how the long-term trend differ from the short-term trend.

Using a two-year chart with a 200 day moving average, you can see that the long-term trend of INTC changed only once. The buy-and-hold investor could have confidently rode out the dips along the way knowing that the long-term trend was still intact.

If you use the moving average as your guide, you can easily spot the trend in an index or stock. Once you know the trend, it's easier to pick the right strategy and take advantage of it.

## Don't Fight the Trends

♦ Uptrends – Buy stock/calls

♦ Sideways – Hold/Sell options

♦ Downtrends – Short stock/ buy puts

**Indicators are NOT more important than trends!**

Here are some strategies to employ during the different trends you might see in the market:

- When the trend is up, choose bullish strategies, like buying stock or call options.

- When the trend is sideways, hold onto your present investments and consider option-selling strategies that generate income during these trendless times in the market.

- If the market is trending down, use bearish strategies, like buying puts or shorting stock in order to capitalize on the trend.

A note about technical indicators: I love to use technical indicators to help me make timing decisions on my investments. My company's web site has some unique color-coded arrows to help me identify the breakouts and breakdowns in a stock as measured by a host of commonly used technical indicators. As I read the emails from my company's thousands of students, I get the impression that many want to trust technical indicators more than trends. This is a dangerous thing to do. Trends should always be given a higher priority in your decision-making process than technical indicators.

Look back at the last few poor investments you've made and see if you made the mistake of ignoring the trend over another piece of information. I'll bet you'll find that the majority of stocks you lost money on were ones you bought when the trend was down. You can't expect to make money if you're trying to swim against the current. The current always wins.

Here are a couple of graphs to illustrate this fact. I've combined the graphs of Cisco Systems as well as Applied Materials and with the NASDAQ Composite Index. Notice how the highs and lows of these market leaders correspond to the entire NASDAQ market. Hopefully you're starting to see what I mean when I say the trend is your friend.

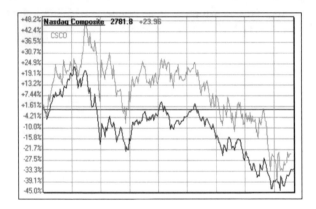

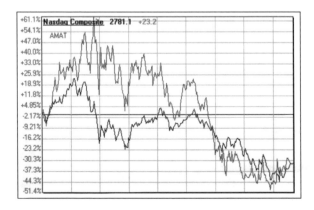

In a moment I'm going to give you a simple three-step process for screening stocks using trends, but first I want to teach you an important lesson.

Moving averages are probably the most simple, yet under utilized indicator in the investing world. I consider a moving average an indispensable piece of information for any investment decision. The moving average can help us identify the trend as well as determine areas of support and resistance. These are critical pieces of information.

Here's the graph of Intel we looked at earlier. I want you to look at it again and notice how the stock seems to bounce off the moving average. Notice which way it bounces when the stock is trending up and which way it bounces when the stock is trending down.

Can you see how the stock bounces up when the trend is up and down when the trend is down?

The stock and the moving average are in love ... they constantly want to move together. When they come together, there is either going to be a breakout or a breakdown. I like to use technical indicators to help me determine which will happen. When the stock and moving average come together and the indicators show bullish signals, I play for a bounce up. When the indicators are showing bearish signals, I expect a bounce down.

It's when you try to mix trends and signals that you get into trouble. The indicators showed bullish signals when the stock was trending down the last two months on this graph, but each rally hit the moving average and fell back.

These are what are commonly called "Bear Traps." They looked like a bullish breakout, but quickly changed and trapped those who placed bullish trades in a bad situation. This is just like a correction in a bullish market, but in reverse. We know the market corrects every once in a while in a bullish market, so why would it not do the same in a bearish one?

In a bullish market, the dips represent great buying opportunities. You've probably heard the "buy the dip" approach to investing. Over the past several years it's been a great approach. But if you apply the buy-the-dip approach in a bear market, you're going to find yourself on the wrong side of the market more often than not.

Let's see if I can't reduce this whole discussion into something concise that you can use. Here's what I've come up with:

*When a stock approaches its moving average, it tends to bounce away from the moving average in the direction of the trend of the moving average.*

This rule can help you avoid the bear traps in a down market and find confidence in the bounces during a bull market. Now that you understand this concept, let me give you three simple rules that can help you apply this concept properly. I'm going to take the bullish side of things, as that's the approach most investors tend to favor.

1. Only invest in stocks with an uptrending short-term moving average.

2.   Only invest when the technical indicators you follow give you a bullish signal.

3.   Only invest if there is no immediate overhead resistance on the chart.

I follow these simple rules when I'm looking for investments in a volatile or bear market. It makes me very selective and keeps me on the sidelines when the current is strong.

I put the trend at the top of the list and then I look at the indicators. I check to make sure there is no resistance to stop a rally. If I see there is a previous high or an area of congestion just above the current price, I will either pass on the trade or wait until the stock is able to close above this level before investing in it.

Shorter-term investors may see opportunities to play the bear traps with calls or buying stock. Doing this is both risky and aggressive, but if you're going to do it, get in the play when the indicators turn positive and use the downtrending moving average or any overhead resistance as your exit target. If you use this risky short-term approach, be sure to get out quickly and not hold past these exit targets.

Volume usually increases in support of a change in the trend. When the moving average starts pointing up, look for volume to increase on the up days in the market or the individual stock. If volume is weak or dropping, be very cautious or simply avoid the trade. It's just the opposite on the downside. Look for volume to increase on the down days and dwindle on the up days. This indicates support of the trend.

Let's finish off our discussion of trends by looking at some specific stocks and applying our three-step screening process. The first stock we'll evaluate is Intel.

Intel had a dramatic selloff shortly after an analyst lowered his rating and earnings estimate on the company. Nobody wanted to believe this young analyst and many thought he was crazy for downgrading a market bellwether like Intel. This took place in the first week in September.

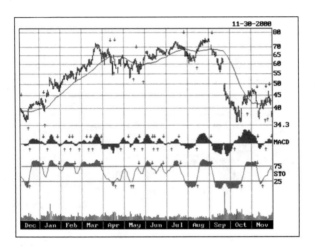

Just prior to this report in mid August, INTC had fallen below its moving average and then staged a nice rally from the low 60's to the mid 70's. This dip and subsequent rally sucked a tremendous amount of new money into INTC stock as investors used the "buy the dip" approach. If we applied the three-step process I just taught you, could we have avoided this stock and the eventual collapse? Let's see.

Notice that the breakdown through the moving average at the beginning of August helped to flatten out the moving average from the uptrend it had been in. At the time the stock began to rally, the trend of the moving average was clearly flat. This, alone, should have made you more cautious if you hadn't abandon the stock altogether. But let's say you saw a very strong breakout signal in the indicators and decided to play anyway. The final thing would have been to check the resistance.

Notice how the stock had twice before gotten just above $70 and then fallen back. If we were going to play this stock at that time, we would have chosen $70 as our exit target, which would have easily gotten us out with a profit before the analysts' downgrade hit the stock.

Now with the trend clearly down, we would have to patiently wait for the stock to rally enough to turn the moving average positive before even considering another bullish trade on INTC.

The next stock we want to look at is Oracle. Let's focus again around the end of August.

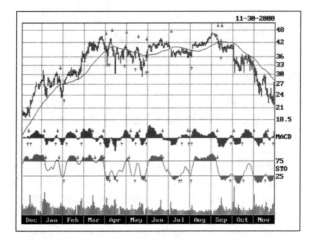

Notice that the stock was above the moving average at that time and the moving average was clearly pointing up. This is good. If we're looking to buy stock or call options, this is exactly what we like to see. Now we go to step two.

The stock moves close to its moving average the first week in September. This is where we would look for a breakout in the form of a bounce up or a breakdown. We look at the indicators to help us decide which direction the stock might go. Notice that the indicators all clearly turned negative in the first week in September just as the stock was also bouncing lower off resistance at the previous high from last March. This is easily enough to keep us out of the stock. The indicators are negative and the stock has hit resistance. This time it's a breakdown that sends the stock to its lows for the year.

The failed rally at the end of September is a classic bear trap, one that would have made a great put option play. This would be a good example to look at when we get to our discussion of "Puts for Profit" later in this book.

Let's do one more example. This final graph is for Tyco. This is an old economy stock that has not been hit quite so hard in the bear market of 2000. Let's focus our attention on the far right side of the graph, as that is the present time.

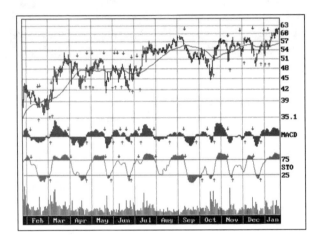

Overall, the trend of the stock has been up, but there have been several short periods of sideways movement, as well. One of these was in the month of December. The stock crossed back and forth over the moving average several times during November and December. Right near the end of December the stock crossed the moving average and the indicators turned positive again. However, since the trend was still not positive, it was a time to be cautious.

There is also very strong resistance at about $60 that the stock has not been able to pass on numerous prior attempts. This would be an example of a stock we could watch. It appears as if the trend will turn positive, but we need to wait until the stock clears the overhead resistance before investing. (You can see that the stock eventually moved past the resistance and continued up. Patience would have been rewarded.)

Now that you understand how to recognize and use trends, let's see how you can incorporate them into your investment program. As I mentioned at the start of this chapter on trends, I like to check the trends of the market, leading sectors, and individual stocks before investing my money.

To assist me in this process, my company created a Market Posture Report on its web site. This is basically an area that displays a thumbnail image of the major market indexes and the leading sector indexes so we can determine the trends and spot strong sectors.

You can easily do this on almost any financial web site that offers charting, but you'll have to look at each chart individually. Having them all in one place just makes it faster and easier to complete this job.

Here's an example of the Market Posture Report taken from the Investor Toolbox web site.

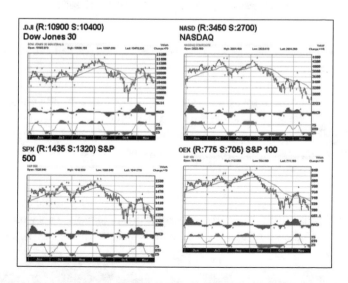

Using the moving average, it's easy to spot the trend from these four major market indexes. This clearly shows a downtrend in the market. If you are a bullish investor, you would know today is a perfect day for a round of golf. If you are a bearish investor, you would begin your search for bearish investments. Even in the most bearish market conditions, there always seems to be one or two sectors that perform well. This is a result of money rotating from the weak sectors into the more stable ones.

A quick look at some of the leading sector index graphs can help you identify where the money is rotating. If you're interested in playing the upside in a down market, you should at least focus your attention to the strongest performing sectors.

Here's a short list of some of the leading sectors with their index symbols. I like to instruct the students in my workshops to create a portfolio of these indexes so they can easily track the indexes movements and spot the changes in their trends.

## Major Sector Indexes

| | |
|---|---|
| Dow Jones Industrial Average | DJI |
| S&P 500 | SPX |
| S&P 100 | OEX |
| Nasdaq 100 | NDX |
| Russell 2000 | RUT |
| Internet | INX |
| Semiconductor | SOX |
| Computers | XCI |
| Software | CWX |
| Networking | NWX |
| Morgan Stanley Hi Tech | MSH |
| Banking | BIX |
| Broker Dealer | XBD |
| Healthcare | HCX |
| Pharmaceutical | DRG |
| Insurance | IUX |
| Oil | OIX |
| Retail | RLX |
| Airline | XAL |

Become a student of the trends and you'll find that you will become a more selective investor. You'll be more patient and emotions will not have such a big impact on your decisions.

To summarize, let's review our three-step evaluation process:

---

## Three Keys to Success

♦ Only invest in uptrending stocks in uptrending sectors

♦ Only invest when technical indicators you follow give you a bullish signal

♦ Only invest if there is NO immediate overhead resistance—like a moving average or a previous high or area of congestion

---

If you want to avoid the bear traps and stay on the sidelines until the trend changes, sticking to these simple rules will help you.

Just avoid downtrending stocks altogether and you should see a dramatic improvement in your results. Don't become a bottom fisher trying to buy depressed stocks in hopes of a recovery. These stocks are weak for a reason and have a good chance of getting even weaker. Find strong stocks in uptrends. In some respects, you might need to throw out one of the oldest sayings in the market: "buy low and sell high." A better approach would be to "buy high and sell higher."

Use technical indicators on uptrending stocks to time your entry and exit. Longer-term investors should use longer-term indicators. Recognize that nearly every popular indicator is a lagging indictor and will rarely get you in at the very start of a new trend. These indicators also won't help you get out at the very top, but they generally do a good job of getting you a nice chunk out of the middle of each trend. Be satisfied with that, and you'll steer clear of many pitfalls that can reduce your returns.

Finally, be aware of resistance. That's the ceiling area where stocks tend to bounce lower. The more often a stock hits a certain price and falls back, the stronger the area of resistance becomes. It will usually take a rally on higher volume to finally get through these areas and establish a new trend.

If you see overhead resistance on an otherwise strong looking stock, just be patient and wait for the stock to break through the resistance and close at a higher price. All you're usually doing when you wait like this is missing out on the first few dollars of potential. If you're shooting for the chunk in the middle, you're not too late.

# Chapter Three

# Stops

Whenever I do a workshop or speak in front of a large group of investors, I always ask them, "How many of you, looking back at the investments you made in the last year, could have done 1, 2, maybe 3 percent better on your whole portfolio by eliminating one or two really bad investments?" I don't ask them to hold up their hands because it can be kind of embarrassing for some. But I do look out and see almost all of their heads nodding in agreement—much like some of you reading this book are doing right now.

Investing is kind of like the game of golf to me. I consider myself to be a pretty decent golfer, although my score does not always reflect this. I can play a pretty good round of golf and then have one disastrous hole. That one disastrous hole can mess up my whole score, leaving me with a score that doesn't reflect the fact that I played 17 good holes.

If I can help each of you eliminate that one really bad trade you seem to make each year from your portfolio, I will have succeeded. And that might help you to do another 1, 2, or 3 percent better each and every year. Can you imagine the difference of having that extra 1or 2 percent, and having it compound over a lifetime of investing? What difference might that extra money make when you reach retirement age and have it to use to live on? It's the little things that often have a huge impact down the road.

If you asked any investor who has taken a catastrophic loss on an investment if they had ever intended to take that large of a loss, they would almost certainly say, "never." You see, it's an easy decision to make when you first get into a new investment. But it's a whole different story when the investment has already dropped 10 or 20 percent.

This is one of the most common mistakes investors make, and it's an easy one to avoid. The solution to this problem is to begin using stop loss orders to protect your investments from sudden dramatic declines. The time to start is with your next investment. Stops are the easiest way to avoid taking one of those cata-strophic losses ever again. How much could that simple change save you over a lifetime of investing?

A stop loss order is an order you give your stockbroker to sell your investment if it hits a certain price you have set as your "get-out point." The order is typically given to the broker at the time the initial purchase is made, or right after. This is when emotions are least likely to cloud your judgment.

Stop loss orders can be placed as a Good Til Cancelled order (GTC) so that it stays in place until it either triggers and fills, or is cancelled by you or your broker. Most firms will keep a GTC order in their system for about 60 days before it automatically cancels. You will need to check the policies at your brokerage firm to make sure you know exactly how they treat GTC stop orders.

So the question is: why don't we use these things? Why don't we put up these safety nets to help protect our portfolios against the unexpected and dramatic declines in the market place? Now I'm sure you will agree that there has been a lot of this lately ... declines in the market, and those of you who understand what a stop loss is and have used it are probably the ones sitting in cash with smiles on your faces waiting for things to get better.

These wise investors have preserved most of the profits they have made over the last year and are now waiting to get back into the market when they see the opportunity present itself again.

Let's talk about stop losses and try to get to the bottom of why people don't use them. Then hopefully you'll get to the point where you can make a personal commitment to incorporate them into your investing approach. It is important that you learn how and when to use them so that they work for your benefit and not for your detriment.

The first thing I want to point out is that we should always have a stop loss. A stop loss is what allows us to go into a trade saying, "I am willing to risk this much money if I'm wrong." This is a decision you need to make when you first get into the trade. In other words, once you get out on the high wire, when you have your money at risk in the market, you want to have a safety net already in place.

The time to decide how much we want to risk is when we are optimistic ... when we think things are going to work out to our benefit. Let's face it, you're not going to get into a new investment unless you see some opportunity. The time is not after you get in and the thing starts moving, maybe even in the opposite direction you expected. The time to set a stop loss is when you have made the decision to get into a stock. This will take away the worries such as: "What if I'm wrong? What if I'm making a mistake right now getting into this investment? How much am I prepared to lose?"

I am going to give you some guidelines right now, but there is nothing carved in stone on this subject. You have to individually decide what you are willing to risk. Some of you are going to be more aggressive and be able to risk a larger portion of what you invest. Others of you will be very conservative, and may wish to go to the conservative side of these ranges.

You may notice that I won't be giving you just one number. That is not the purpose of this discussion. I don't want you to do this strategy the way Ross does it or the way someone else does it.

You need to decide what's best for you. Investing is a very personal thing and everyone needs to have an approach that fits their personality and their individual lifestyle.

For stock, I want to give you the range of 10 to 20 percent of the initial purchase price. One of the really great books on basic investing principles—one that I think would make a nice addition to anyone's investment library—is a book called, *How to Make Money in Stocks*, by William O'Neil. He is the founder of *Investors Business Daily* (IBD) newspaper. This book is a wonderful resource for new investors to learn a proven approach to investing in stocks. The entire IBD newspaper is built around a simple approach called the CANSLIM method for selecting stocks.

One of the things Mr. O'Neil points out in his book is that we should all use stop losses. In his book, he recommends a 7 to 8 percent range for a stop loss on a stock. Now that is what I would consider a very tight stop, but if you are not willing to accept a lot of risk, it works well. So that is one approach.

I personally like the range of 10 to 20 percent. I would say that, for the most part, if you buy a stock and it drops 20 percent before you are able to realize any kind of a profit, you have probably made a mistake in buying that stock at the time you did. And when this happens, you need to come to grips with reality and take action to preserve your capital.

It's hard for most investors to realize they have a better chance of earning back a loss on their next trade than sticking with the current one in hopes that it turns around. The problem we make is that once we have a stock go bad, we want to make sure we earn back that loss on that stock, and that's not always the best decision. The better way is to preserve your capital and use the tools and resources you have at your disposal to find another investment that gives you the opportunity to make money and offset that loss. That may not be in the same stock you're currently in. It may be in a totally different investment.

Many an investor has met his/her demise waiting for that sure winner to turn around. More often than not, you will keep waiting for that stock to come back, and it never does. When you finally accept this, you're looking at one of those catastrophic losses—30, 40, or 50 percent that will bring down the total return of your entire portfolio.

The natural tendency for someone who has suffered that kind of catastrophic loss is to go back in and say, "Now I need to apply this more aggressive strategy," or "Now I need to buy call options to make it back that much faster." Doing this usually just compounds the problem and you end up creating an even worse loss than you had in the first place.

If you're an options investor, I would suggest a stop loss range of 30 to 50 percent of the premium paid for the option. Thirty percent is actually very close for an option trade. Since a small movement in a stock can create a much larger percentage move in an option premium, you need to allow a bit more room with options than with stocks. Keep in mind that you have already limited your total risk to the premium you pay, which is usually a small fraction of the price of a share of stock. This being the case, you have to be willing to risk a larger portion of this premium in order to keep you from getting stopped out too early.

Another challenge for the options investors is that most brokers are not going to accept any kind stop loss order on an option, and those that do—at least most I've come across—will only accept it as a day order. Your only option in this case may be to use a mental stop. (We'll talk about this more in a minute). Only at firms that specifically cater to option investors will you usually find a policy that allows GTC stop orders on options. Some live brokers will offer this service to good clients, but generally you will give them your stop price and then trust that they will be following your position close enough to enter the order to get you out when your trigger price is reached. Those who operate like this will almost certainly warn you in advance that you're not guaranteed your stop price. It's kind of their way of saying, "I may not be watching that close." Not much comfort if you've got your hard-earned money on the line.

A day order will only last for one trading day and then it automatically expires. In order to replace your stop order, you have to re-enter it the next morning or you won't have the comfort of knowing your safety net is in place.

It doesn't cost anything to place or change a stop order. One of the biggest myths in investing is that brokers get paid a commission to "take" an order. In reality, brokers only get paid a commission to "fill" an order. A stop order only costs you money if it is executed, and this is an order we place in hopes of it never getting filled. If you place a stop and it gets filled, you are most likely going to be happy to be out of that losing investment with part of your capital. Your commission is a small price to pay for that kind of protection. Think of a stop loss order as not having to pay to put up the safety net, but having to pay if you ever land in it. I think you get the point.

Some people who trade where only day stop orders are allowed get tired of the hassle of changing or re-entering those stop orders each and every day. In other words, they get lazy and they stop using them. Most option investors end up keeping their stops in their heads as a mental stop. Let's define this term right now.

A mental stop is something we keep in our head. We decide where we want to cut our losses and then we monitor our position and physically enter the sell order ourselves when that price is reached. There is nothing automated about it and it requires constant monitoring.

For those who choose to use mental stops, I've found it very helpful to write down your desired trigger point in some type of trading journal or trade record. It just seems that writing it down makes it more real and makes it easier to react to when the stop price is reached. That's the real weakness of a mental stop. You have to be disciplined enough to physically place the order to sell when you're emotions are probably at their peak. If you find after trying a mental stop you simply don't have the discipline to pull the trigger and get out, you should probably avoid those fast-moving or volatile investments that often result in having to make this type of decision at some point.

A trading journal or trading record is a good idea for most investors. It's is a great way to keep track of your trades and focus on the decisions you make and why. It's also good to record the current market conditions at the time you make each trade. You can write down the closing figures for the major indexes and any major news events of the day.

A journal is also helpful for looking back at mistakes you might have made and seeing if perhaps you had a flaw in your decision-making process. Most of us can hardly remember doing a trade ... let alone what motivated us to do it. If you decide to use a trading journal, write down in it what you have set as your stop price each time you enter a new position. It's amazing how when you write something down it becomes so much more real. They often say that a goal not written is only a wish. The same can probably be said of stop loss orders. You need to have them written down or placed with your broker, or they are no more than just a wish. Usually if you write your stop price down, you will become more disciplined, and it will keep you constantly reminded of what it is.

The next thing we are going to look at is other ways to determine where to put a stop. Most people who don't use stops will tell you that they hate getting stopped out of an investment only to see it almost instantly rise again above their stop price. We call this getting "whipsawed," and it's something that you will eventually have to deal with if you use stops. So let's look at another way to determine where to place our stops to allow the best opportunity to stay in an investment even if it dips.

We talk a lot in the trend chapter in this book about support and resistance. Support is an area where buyers of a stock tend to jump in and offset the selling pressure to stabilize the stock. This is a great area to place a stop. It's usually when a stock finally breaks through these areas of support that they have those big drops in price. Setting your stop at this level or slightly below it will help you get out before everyone starts rushing for the exit.

Another great way to determine where to place a stop is to follow the trend of a stock and get out when the trend is broken. If you're going to use the trends as a signal to exit a position, you first need to decide how you're going to measure and track it. We get into this in great detail in the chapter on trends, but let me tell you that one of the simplest ways to track a trend is by looking at the simple moving average.

You should select a moving average to use that matches the time frame of your investment objective. A person playing short-term moves would most likely want to follow a 30 or 50-day moving average, whereas a person wishing to invest for the long haul and ride out the small dips would most likely use a longer-term moving average, like a 200 day. Match the moving average to your objectives.

If you are watching a stock and you see that the stock has moved through its moving average, this would be a great time to move to the sidelines. Many investors who use mental stops like to set their stops at the moving average they choose to follow. They know that if the stock breaks through their moving average, they need to place the order to get out.

Those of you who like to hold an investment for a long period of time and ride out the dips will need to use a longer-term moving average to avoid stopping yourself out before the stock is finished running. Every investor should be aware of the long-term trend of their investments and be able to recognize when these trends change or breakdown.

The easiest way to see this—for those of you who are in more of that long-term perspective with your investments—is to look at a long-term chart. By long term I mean more than one year. Use a three-year, five-year, or ten-year chart and apply a 200-day moving average to it. This will give you a nice long-term trend to follow. Notice that many of the stocks you look at will be way above the moving average for long periods of time. This will make it so that you are not panicking at each little dip that happens along the way. But when it finally does break the 200-day moving average, (which is commonly looked at as a long-term level of support for a stock), that might be the time to say, "That's enough" and to move to the sidelines while you look for another investment to put those funds into.

Look at the following two graphs. One is a one-year graph of Sun Microsystems with a 30-day moving average and the other is a five-year graph with a 200-day moving average.

**One-year graph with 30-day moving average**

**Five-year graph with 200-day moving average**

The shorter-term investor using the one-year graph and the 30-day moving average would have moved in and out of the stock several times over the year shown. The longer-term investor using the five-year chart and 200-day moving average would have made far fewer moves and stayed in the stock for most of the upward trend.

Finally, I sense some confusion in some of the emails I get from past students in regards to the difference between a stop order and a stop limit order. Many of the online brokers actually have two buttons you can click on their order screens that say "STOP" or "STOP LIMIT." When most investors look at this screen, the word "stop" jumps out at them. They don't stop to think what the difference between the two is.

In fact, some people reason that since they are going to put a price where they want the safety net to be, that is their stop limit, and they click the box that says stop limit and enter the price that they want to get out at.

Now let me just make the clarification so there is no fogginess on this issue, because it is very important. A stop loss order and a stop limit order are two very different things. And it is very important that you understand the difference so you don't use the wrong one.

I am going to make a blanket statement and then I'll explain it so that you will understand why I'm saying it. Here is the simple rule: DO NOT USE A STOP LIMIT, just don't do it. What you want to use is a stop order or a stop loss order. (A safety net order.)

So what's the difference? In this case, one single word can totally change the meaning of what you're doing. Let's look at the difference.

Let's say we buy a stock for $20 and that we are willing to risk 20% of that. This means that the stock could drop down to $16 before we would get out. So this is where we place our stop loss order to get us out. If our broker will allow us, we would place our order good til canceled (GTC) to keep it in place without having to re-enter it on a daily basis.

The thing that would trigger our stop order is a drop in the price of the stock to $16 or less. When the $16 price is reached, at anytime the market is open, our order is triggered. The brokerage firm then sends a *market order* to the exchange that is filled at the current market price.

That doesn't necessarily mean you are going to get out at $16; it just means that when the stock hits $16, the brokerage house will send a market order in to get you out at whatever the market price is when your order arrives. This may be a little above or a little below the $16, but it is the $16 price that triggered the market order being sent.

Now, how is this different than the stop limit order? First, it's important that you understand what a limit order is. This can be an order to buy or sell an investment where we set the minimum price we're willing to accept. This price is our limit. A limit order is not filled unless you are able to get your limit price or a better price. So let's apply this to a stop order, as we understand it thus far.

Let's use the same example of the $20 stock with a stop at $16. Remember, our intent is to get out if the price drops to $16 or lower. If we set a stop limit at $16, and the stock goes down and hits $16, instead of a market order being sent to the exchange to sell our stock, a *limit order* to sell our stock at $16 or better is sent. The order to sell won't be filled unless you are able to get $16 or better, which in this case would be a higher price. If the market for the investment doesn't trade at or above your limit price, the order is not filled. So why is this important?

Let's assume the stock we own has traded down to $16.50 from the $20 price we bought at. Then overnight, while the market is closed, the company announces a shortfall in their earnings. The next morning the stock opens up at $14. This is what is called a gap down. The opening price is lower than the previous day's close, leaving a gap in the price chart.

In this case, our stop limit order would be triggered once the stock traded below $16 and our limit order to sell would be sent to the exchange. But since the stock is no longer trading at or above $16, it would not be filled. If the stock continues to drop, we would continue to lose more money.

Can you see how you are stuck? You have an order in—you put up the safety net—but by selecting a stop limit order rather than a traditional stop order, you specified that you are only willing to accept a sell price of $16 or better.

If you are going to use a stop as a safety net to sell out of an investment at a certain price, you should always use a traditional stop order and not a stop limit order. Think of them as a stop market and stop limit and it will help you to understand what the difference is. This will make your order go in as a market order and not a limit order.

A stop limit order is typically used as a buying order, not a selling order. An investor may want to buy into a stock after it reaches a certain price they've determined to constitute a new breakout, but they don't want to buy if it doesn't reach that price. They use a buy stop limit order to trigger their order at that certain price and that then assures them of that price or better. This is not an order to be used by the novice investor. Experienced investors who clearly understand what they are trying to accomplish and recognize the stop limit order as the vehicle to help them are typically the only ones who use this type of order.

So let's review the simple rules relating to stops:

- Always set a stop when you enter a new position.

- Use traditional stop loss orders and not stop limit orders.

- Place hard stops with your broker as good til canceled (GTC), if possible.

- If your broker does not allow GTC stop orders, use either day orders or mental stops.

- If you use mental stops, write down the stop price to help you become more disciplined.

- Set your stops on stocks somewhere in the neighborhood of 10 to 20 percent of the purchase price.

- Set your stops on option positions at 30 to 50 percent of the premium paid.

- Never lower a stop loss trigger price from your original stop price.

Everyone always talks about the value of an education. Maybe this example will help you understand a little better what that really means. What if you had known everything we've covered in this chapter on stops and had applied it to the stock that you had your last catastrophic loss on? Would you still be in that stock? How much would you have saved? Hopefully now you understand a little more why stops are important and how easy yet critical they are to use.

Stop losses are very important ... I hope you can now see that. The fact is, money saved by using a stop is just like money earned. All your past catastrophic losses are the price you've paid to learn this hard lesson. Now you'll better understand the cost of education. Nobody would ever get into an investment and plan on taking a 40 to 50 percent loss. So if you ever find yourself in that position after reading this book, you'll have nobody to blame but that guy or gal you see in the mirror each morning.

If you find yourself in that position with one of your current investments, you need to ask yourself this simple question, "If I had the money that this investment is worth today in cash, would

I put it into this same investment?" If the answer is no, then you know what you need to do. Sell and move on.

# Chapter Four

# Buying Puts

In my company's two-day online training workshops, we do not spend a lot of time talking about puts. We want to make sure that we focus on the strategies that are working in the current market environment. But now we're facing a whole different set of circumstances and it's important to introduce you to some additional strategies and tools.

In this chapter I'd like to help you understand how to use put options to protect your portfolio and to profit from falling stock prices.

A put option is the right to sell stock at a set price for a set period of time. In a sense, buying a put option contract locks in a selling price (the strike price of the put) for 100 shares of the underlying stock. That price must be honored by the seller of the put no matter how much lower the price of the stock is at expiration.

It's important that you understand that you don't need to actually own shares of the underlying stock to buy a put on that stock. You can buy a put on any optionable stock and profit if the price of the stock drops below the strike price of that put.

We have talked about selling puts to generate income as an equivalent strategy to covered calls. This is a bullish strategy involving puts that is used when the market is trending up. Now we are going to focus on the strategy of buying puts.

As I mentioned before, the two primary uses of put options are to insure your stocks against falling prices and to profit from falling prices on stocks you don't own. The first strategy is to use a put option as an insurance policy. We call that a protective put on stocks we already own.

The second reason to use put options is to profit or to speculate on falling prices for stocks or indexes ... or whatever investment vehicle we are using.

---

## Buying Put Options

♦ Protective puts (insurance policy)

♦ Speculating on falling prices

---

Above are the two primary ways to use puts. I think it is very important for you to understand that you can use an option to protect yourself. This is the primary reason options were created in the first place. They were created to be used as hedges—to protect an investment portfolio against losses or unexpected movements.

Mutual fund managers and other professionals understand the importance of hedging against losses. They look to the options market during times of high market volatility to inexpensively insure their portfolios against the unexpected. These very same tools and strategies the professionals use to insure their portfolios are available to the individual investor who understands how to use them properly.

So let's take a close look at these; let's break them down and give you some of the tools and resources you need to use puts effectively to either protect yourself in a bear market or to speculate on falling prices.

First, we're going to look at how to use puts for protection and then we will look at how you can use them as a vehicle to profit from falling stock prices.

I want to share with you an example that we use in our two-day online investing workshop. We like to relate option trading to real estate because most of the investors who attend our classes are homeowners, or prospective homeowners, and have a basic grasp of the elements of a simple real estate transaction.

We use an example of a young couple buying their first house using a lease with an option to buy. We assume that the market value of the house goes up during the term of their option and they eventually exercise their right to buy the house at the agreed upon price in their contract. Now they are the proud owners of a home valued at $200,000 in the current market.

I want you to put yourself in this young couple's position. If you're a homeowner, think of the current value of your home. A home is one of the largest investments most people make in their lives and therefore, most homeowners—especially those who have a mortgage—hedge themselves to protect their investment.

Let's use our example of a house worth $200,000. Our objective is to protect and preserve our investment in that house. The traditional way to do this is by purchasing a homeowner's insurance policy.

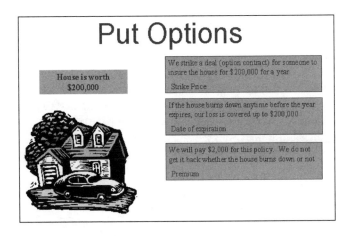

# Put Options

House is worth
$200,000

We strike a deal (option contract) for someone to insure the house for $200,000 for a year

Strike Price

If the house burns down anytime before the year expires, our loss is covered up to $200,000

Date of expiration

We will pay $2,000 for this policy. We do not get it back whether the house burns down or not

Premium

The purpose of an insurance policy is to protect us against events that could cause damage to our home and reduce its value or destroy it completely. This includes things like a hurricane, or a flood, or a fire, or a tornado. Any of these disasters can cause significant damage to your home. If your home were damaged by one of these catastrophes, you would make a claim to the insurance company and they would cover the cost of "putting" your house back to its original condition, as long as the cost were within the predefined limits of your policy. None of this should be too surprising to those of you who have a homeowner's insurance policy. Insurance is one of life's necessary evils.

What you may not realize is that an insurance policy has many of the same features as an option contract. First of all, a policy is basically a contract between you and the insurance company. The face value of the policy is just like the strike price of an option contract. And, just as with insurance, there is a specified time in every policy when it expires and we need to pay a premium to keep the policy in force. Hopefully this is starting to sound familiar.

So to summarize, an insurance policy has a strike price, expiration day, and premium ... just like an option contract. As is the case with an option, the seller of a policy is bound by the terms of the contract and has the obligation to perform in the event of a claim.

An insurance policy is just like a put option because its value increases as the asset it is protecting drops in value. Let's go back to our example of the $200,000 house. Let's say you leave your teenagers at home one day and they happen to leave the iron on face down. The house catches fire and there is $50,000 done in damage. The insurance policy is now worth $50,000 because that's what the insurance company would be obligated to pay on the claim. You would not get your premium back, and you would have to deduct that from the insurance claim to figure your net benefit.

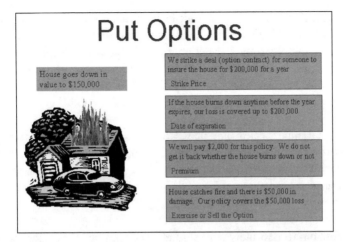

When you buy a put option, you're basically insuring a stock against a fall in price below the strike price of the put you buy. If the stock is lower than that price on expiration day, you can offset the loss in your stock with the profits on your put option. Your profit is the difference between the strike price of the put and the current price of the stock.

If you bought a $70 put option on Cisco for $2 ($200 per contract) and the stock was trading for $65 on expiration day, your put would be worth $5, or $500 per contract, less the premium you paid for the option for a net profit of $3, or $300 per contract.

It's important that you understand that just like with insurance, the premium you pay for an option is non-refundable and must be considered a cost that needs to be deducted from your profits. Another thing to consider is that even if your house doesn't burn down, the insurance company will not give you back your premium. It works the same with the option. The premium you pay for the option is your maximum loss if the stock doesn't move in the direction you need it to go.

Now let's turn the table a little and look at this transaction from the perspective of the insurance company. When they issue a policy, they accept the risk of paying up to the face value of the house if it burns to the ground. That's a huge risk for such a small premium. What's their motivation to take such a big risk? They know there is only a small chance your house will burn down; and considering all the homes they insure, they will easily collect enough premiums to pay those few claims and still have some profit left over.

It's a numbers game they play. Now obviously, it works for them. If you're like me, when you travel to large cities, you can look at the skylines and pick out some of the biggest buildings. It is amazing to see how many of those big buildings have insurance company names on them.

That model definitely works. In essence, they sell the option, collect the premiums, and if the house doesn't burn down, they get to keep it. Also, they know that the majority of people will pay the premiums their entire life, and a small percentage of those people will ever need to make a claim against that policy. What insurance companies basically do is sell puts. It's a great income strategy ... as long as there are no "wildfires" or "hurricanes."

Now all of this doesn't mean we don't want to have insurance. As a homeowner, we shouldn't look at it and think, "Since our house didn't burn down, we don't get anything from our insurance." It gives us peace of mind. It enables us to sleep at night ... just knowing that we are insured.

Do you see how this all works out? That is the beauty of a put option. It's very similar in nature to an insurance policy. The biggest difference when we apply this analogy to stocks is that you don't need to own the house to buy a policy on it. Imagine having a policy on each house in the neighborhood you live in. If one of the neighbor's homes burned down, the insurance company would bring the check to your house. Just the same, you don't need to own a stock to buy a put.

That's the next aspect of put options we're going to look at, buying puts for profits. But first, let's first make sure we understand how to use them for protection.

---

### Protective Puts

♦ Each contract protects 100 shares

♦ Lock in a selling price (strike price)

♦ Must be closed out on or before the expiration day

♦ Offset loss from strike price to current price

♦ Can be bought back if it is no longer needed

---

I want you to mentally replace the house in the previous example with stock. This could be individual stock you've owned or maybe even stock you own right now. Think about some of the stock you have in your portfolio right now. Let's look at how we might be able to protect it. If you don't want to incur any more substantial losses during a bear market, you might consider put options on those stocks that have you worried.

Just keep in mind that we are going to replace the house in the previous example with stock; that should help you keep things straight. All of the terms relating to an insurance policy as you saw here also apply to a put option.

Since put option contracts are based on 100 shares of stock, you need to buy one put for each 100 shares of stock you own to be fully insured. If you have an odd number of shares, you have to decide to either insure more or leave some uninsured as this only works in 100 share multiples.

You also need to determine which strike price to select for your put. You have some discretion here, but I advise you to stay with a strike price that is close to the current price of the stock. I usually like to go with the first strike price below the current price of the stock. Let's look at an example.

Let's say you own 100 shares of Microsoft trading at $70 per share and you are worried that the company might miss their next earnings estimate. You want to insure yourself against a decline in the stock if they do, so you purchase puts. When you look at the available put option contracts for the current month, you see the closest ones are the $70 and $65 contracts. The higher the strike price of the put, the more expensive it is.

The other thing that impacts the premium you pay for your put is the time until expiration. The longer until expiration, the more expensive the option is. I recommend going out two to three months for protective puts. This reduces the impact of time decay on your premium and gives you more solid protection.

In this example, let's assume you chose the $65 contract that expires in two months for your insurance. Let's say the premium at the time is $2, or $200 per contract. Now you are insured against any decline in MSFT beyond $65 from today until the expiration day of that option. The first $2 of the drop in price is like your deductible. Let's see how the protective put will reduce your loss on a drop in the stock to $60.

---

### MSFT Drops from $70 to $60

- ◆ Original price of stock        $70

- ◆ Current price of stock        $60

- ◆ Loss on stock        $10

- ◆ Gain from $65 put option        $5

- ◆ Net Loss        $5 (plus $2 premium)

---

Once you reach the point where you've covered the deductible and passed the strike price, the put option will provide dollar-for-dollar protection on any further decline in the stock.

Look at the results of the same play if the stock continues to drop lower. Notice that although the stock drops another $10, the net loss is exactly the same.

---

## MSFT Drops from $70 to $50

♦ Original price of stock      $70

♦ Current price of stock      $50

♦ Potential loss      $20

♦ Gain from $65 put option      $15

♦ Net Loss      $5 (plus $2 premium)

---

Let's go back to the insurance example so I can make another important point. You can select the deductible for your policy when you buy it, which can have a dramatic impact on your premium. It's no different with protective puts. The difference between the price of the stock and the strike price of your protective put is just like your deductible. You have to assume that loss before the policy kicks in and covers anything beyond that. The larger the deductible is (lower put strike price), the cheaper the premium.

In the MSFT example above, you could have selected the $70 put and paid a higher premium to have insurance in place for every dollar the stock dropped below the strike price. In this example, that would have offered 100% protection aside from the premium you paid for the stock.

The biggest difference between protective puts and insurance policies is that you can buy back the protective puts once you don't need them anymore. If you decide you only need insurance until the earnings on MSFT come out, as soon as the news is out, you can close out the put by selling it in the option market at the current price. This will help you recoup some of your premium. With protective puts, you only need pay for what insurance you use. It's a great benefit.

Maybe it would help to look at protective puts another way. Let's say a hurricane has been forecasted on the weather report ... that it is going to hit in a week or so. I'm going to buy an insurance policy to protect my assets against the hurricane. However, the hurricane comes without incident. Once it's gone, I don't want to continue paying that premium anymore. With a homeowner's policy I'm pretty well locked in, but not with a "put" policy. I can simply say, "Hey, I don't see the need for hurricane insurance anymore," and I can cash in my policy right then for whatever portion of the premium is still available at that time.

After you buy a protective put, the premium fluctuates with the movement of the stock and the passing of time. The premium naturally shrinks with the passing of time, but falls faster if the stock falls in price. If the stock rises, the value of a put goes down. You can monitor the current price on the Internet to see what you can recoup anytime before expiration.

If you hold the option until expiration, you have the right to "PUT" 100 shares for each contract you own to another investor and be paid the strike price of the put for your stock. If you "exercise" your put option, that's exactly what will happen. Most brokers do this automatically if the stock is lower than the strike price of the protective put. If you don't want to sell your stock, you need to sell the put in the market some time prior to the end of trading on expiration day. The proceeds will help you offset the loss you will have on your stock position, but allow you to retain the stock to sell at a later date.

If you use protective puts as insurance, you may even find your-self wishing your stock would fall because you know you're insured. About the worst case scenario is that you buy a protective put and the stock goes up or stays the same. You'll lose the premium you paid, which will, in a sense, increase your cost basis on the stock. But if it means you sleep better at night, it's worth it. It's no different than insuring your house and not having it burn down. You don't get your premium back, but at least you have peace of mind.

The final thing I want to mention before we move on to "Puts for Profit" is that you can use protective puts on an entire portfolio just as easily as on individual stocks. Since many indexes have options traded on them, you can use these puts as insurance on a basket or portfolio of stocks. The new NASDAQ index shares, the QQQ, has options which offer a simply way to hedge a technology heavy portfolio. This is just another thing to consider when you feel insurance is needed.

So let's summarize what we've learned about protective puts.

---

## Key Points

♦ Buy protective puts 2-3 months away from expiration

♦ Buy out-of-the-money puts (lower strike than the stock); this is your deductible

♦ Sell the put before expiration, if it is no longer needed, to recover some of the premium

♦ Exercise the put if you want to actually sell shares you own

---

The first key point is to buy a little bit of time. Options are like ice cubes ... always melting. The closer an option gets to expiration, the faster it melts. So it's important for you to understand that by going out to future months for your insurance, you are subjecting yourself a little less to the natural decay of time that takes place with any option. It will cost you a little more money, but it's usually money well spent. Remember, the fastest time decay is taking place in that last month right before expiration.

This is especially true if you only intend to hold the protective put for a short time. Buying the shortest term option saves you a little money upfront, but it doesn't allow you the luxury of changing your mind without incurring another commission and buying more time in a new put option. The time value as it decays going forward will have less of an impact on your positions than if you would have bought the two or three-week period. So generally, look at going out two to three months. You can certainly go out longer than that, but that's up to you to decide based on your individual forecast and how long you want to be protected with this protective put.

Usually you want to buy out-of-the-money puts. This basically means you want to buy put options that are lower than the current price of the stock. Give yourself a little deductible; be willing to take a little bit of risk in the stock declining in value from its present price.

I like to go to the next strike price below the current price of the stock. If I'm really worried about a drop and want to fully insure myself, I may buy the at-the-money put option.

By selecting an out-of-the-money put, you lower the cost of the insurance policy. Remember, the further down you go from the current price, the more your protective put becomes like catastrophic insurance. The premium is small, but the coverage only kicks in if there is a tremendous selloff in the stock. It's like having a big deductible to pay before the coverage kicks in. These are decisions you have to make based on your personal forecast for the individual stocks you play.

Next, we don't need to hold a protective put until expiration day if we no longer need the insurance. And if we don't need the insurance anymore, we can sell the put before it expires (as long as it's no longer needed), and recover a small portion of our premium. The longer you wait, the less the option is going to be worth. If you wait until a day or two before expiration to cash it in, don't be surprised if it is worth hardly anything. It may not even be worth enough to cover the cost of commission to sell. In that case, you may as well let it expire just in case there is a dramatic drop right before expiration day.

If you need insurance for a few days only—like to protect yourself from what could happen after an earnings announcement comes out—just buy the protective put before the announcement and sell it after you've had a chance to see how the announcement impacts the stock. If the stock price drops dramatically, you know you're protected. If it doesn't move at all or moves up, simply sell your put option and recover part of your premium.

Don't be surprised if the premium shrinks very quickly after an earnings announcement. Volatility is a key component of an option's price and volatility is at its peak during times like these ... when many investors are speculating on the earnings release. As soon as the earnings announcement is out, the volatility often collapses, no matter which direction the stock goes. This almost instantly reduces the premiums on the options for that stock, including the put options. So move quick if you decide you want to get out of your protective put.

Finally, if you hold your protective put until expiration day and see that the stock is now lower than your strike price, you need to take some action if you do not want to sell your stock. If you feel the bad times are over for this stock and now you want to hold it for an upward run, you need to close out your put by selling it on or before the close of trading on expiration day. Any profit from the sell of the protective put will help to offset the paper loss on your stock. So you'll be back in the black that much sooner if the stock really does take off again.

Now let's look at how to use puts to profit in a falling market.

Remember a few paragraphs ago when I said that you do not have to own the stock to buy a put option on it? That being the case, investors wishing to profit from falling stock prices are always on the lookout for weak stocks that have the potential to fall. Unfortunately, many of us need only look to our own portfolio to find these kinds of stocks in ... abundance.

You can literally buy a put option on any stock with options listed. You will profit if that stock falls below the strike price of the put option you buy on or before expiration day.

Like I mentioned previously, this approach to put options is kind of like buying insurance on your neighbor's house and hoping it burns down so the insurance company will bring the check to your door. Now obviously, it's a bit morbid to talk about your neighbor's house burning down, but it's an effective way to get you thinking in the right direction.

Let's look at some of the situations that create put buying opportunities. We're going to look at each of these in some detail and then look at a few actual examples.

---

## Buying Puts for Profit
### When to Buy

♦ Downtrending market, sector, stock

♦ Peak in the MACD (the first sign of weakness)

♦ Bounce off the moving average

♦ Shrinking volume

♦ Earnings announcements in a weak market

---

The first thing to consider before buying puts for profit is the trend. It may not sound right, but even in a bear market, the trend is our friend. Knowing what the current trend is will help you determine what investment strategies to consider. When is the best time to buy puts for profit? Obviously, you're going to consider buying puts for profit when the trend of the market, the major sectors, and the stock you're considering playing are down. So what's the best way to determine that?

I like to go to the Market Posture feature on my company's web site at www.investortoolbox.com to check the trends of the market and major sectors before looking for individual stocks. If you are not a subscriber to this service, you can still use some of its features to quickly check the 30-day moving averages on a one-year graph of the major market indexes and the sector index of the sector you're looking at.

Try to find sectors where the index is trending down. These sectors are great places to search for individual put candidates. Once you find a weak sector, you can use the Industry Group Center on the Investor Toolbox to identify the individual stocks that make up that sector or industry group. It's a handy feature to help you narrow your focus to individual stocks.

When I'm looking for potential plays, I look at lots of individual stock charts and pay particular attention to the short-term moving average. If I find one that is pointing down, it becomes a candidate for further analysis.

Trying to find good put plays in a bull market is like trying to find good call plays in a bear market. It's a lot like trying to find a needle in a haystack. For those of you who tried to play call options during the last six months of 2000, you know how difficult this is. Remember, the trend is your friend, so choose strategies that profit in the prevailing trend. When the trend is down, consider buying puts or just stay on the sidelines.

In my seminars, I teach investors to recognize the first sign of weakness in a stock as the exit point for their call option plays. It's this same point that makes a great entry point for a put play. I like to use a Moving Average Convergence Divergence (MACD) histogram to help me spot weakness.

I like to think of the MACD histogram as an indicator that shows the mountains and valleys of a stock. When you buy call options, you should try to time your entry into the position to coincide with the beginning of a new mountain. The ideal exit point is the peak of that mountain. It's very difficult to get out at the very peak, so I tell my students to try to exit as close to the top of the peak as possible.

When buying puts, we want to enter our position just as the stock is beginning to show weakness. Using the MACD histogram, that would also be at or near the peak that is formed when the stock is running up. As the MACD begins to head down, the stock is usually losing ground, which is exactly what we need in order to profit from a put position.

Here's an example of a MACD histogram that clearly shows the kind of peaks I'm speaking of. Notice the two very pronounced peaks in August and again in October that preceded substantial drops in the price of Intel stock.

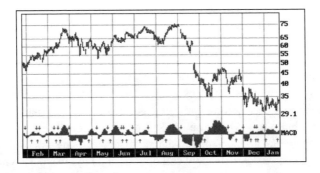

Another sign of weakness is when a weak stock rallies up to its 30-day moving average and then bounces back down. In the chapter on trends, we learned that stocks tend to bounce away from their moving average in the direction of the trend of the moving average. Most downtrending stocks stay below their short-term moving average for much of the downtrends. The short rallies that happen along the way only seem to get the stock back to the moving average where the stock encounters overhead resistance.

Overhead resistance is a powerful force that usually halts the rise in the stock and pushes it back down, following the trend. Just the opposite is true with a rising stock. With the stock above the moving average, each correction along the way takes the stock back to the moving average where it finds support. This is often where the new rally begins as the stock bounces up from this point, following the trend.

In a bullish market, the moving average is a support point where the stock tends to bounce up. In a bearish market, the moving average is a resistance point where the stock tends to bounce down. Remember the simple rule from our discussion earlier in this book on trends: stocks tend to bounce from their moving average in the direction of the trend of their moving average.

So in downtrending stocks, look for a rally toward the moving average when the stock runs out of steam and bounces down. This is commonly referred to as a bear trap because bullish investors buy into these rallies only to be disappointed when the stock hits resistance at the moving average and bounces down again. It's at the peak of these rallies that we like to buy the put.

Another thing to look at is shrinking volume on upward moves. Rallies without volume lack conviction. Low volume rallies are typical in a bear market and serve as traps for the eternally optimistic bulls. It's when you see spikes in volume on the selloffs that you like to play puts. Again, this is just the opposite of everything we learned about call options and buying stock. When we're bullish, we like to see volume increase on the upward movements of the stock. When we play puts, we like to see the volume spike on the downward moves. So volume is another key indicator we follow when screening potential put candidates.

Earnings announcements have become real pivot points for stocks. In a downtrending market it takes more than just good earnings to break the trend. I'm sure you've had the experience of buying a great stock on the expectation of a good earnings announcement, only to see that stock drop after the announcement comes out ... even though it met or beat the analyst estimate. Why does this happen? I've met many investors who love to load up on call options right before an earnings announcement and then can't believe it when their calls get wiped out after a seemingly good earnings report.

You see, it's the buying that makes the stock move. If it's a widely followed stock, like Cisco or AOL, everyone is aware of the earnings dates and the bulls are positioning themselves with stocks and calls to take advantage of it. Nearly everyone who cares gets into the stock prior to the announcement. So when the announcement comes in as expected, there is no one left to buy more stock and push the price higher.

Even though the news was good, the rally runs out of steam and the stock begins to fall as some of those investors who made money on the earnings run begin to take some money off the table. I see it happen all the time.

About the only thing that can extend the earnings run is a blowout announcement that far exceeds the analysts' estimate and surprises the market. While most investors are aware of the analysts' earnings estimate, there is another number that many on Wall Street watch called the "whisper number." Though rarely published, this number is the real number the professionals are expecting the company to top.

This whisper number may be a few pennies higher than the analysts' estimate. A company may beat the analyst number and fall short of the whisper number and get treated as if they had a poor earnings report. When you hear the news, you may think the stock will rise because they beat the estimate, but missing the whisper number results in a selloff.

In a bear market, just meeting the estimate is usually not enough. To overcome the tremendous pull of the downtrend, only a surprise blowout earnings report is going to get the scared investors off the sidelines to spend money on more stock. Earnings announcements in a bear market are a great time to play puts. If you're looking for the slight edge that tilts the scales in your favor, an earnings report might be it.

I am not a huge put player, but this is one time I really like to play these strategies. It feels like I have a little bit of an edge because the tendency for most stocks in a falling market is to continue to fall. There are many investors sitting there waiting for any indication of bad news in that earnings release or in the conference call that follows. If investors sense any hesitation on the part of management in their forecasts for the next quarter earnings report, look out below. It doesn't matter if they just reported a record quarter; the stock is going to get hammered.

If you play puts on earnings announcements in a bear market, there is a chance that the company will miss the estimate all together. This is where the big money in puts is made ... and it's

made very fast. One of my good friends often tells of the time
when fathers took their sons to the woodshed to give them spank-
ings when they were bad. He relates this to a stock after the company misses an earnings estimate to "being taken to the woodshed." I think you get the picture. It's usually not pretty, unless
you're holding a bunch of put option contracts ... then it's like
Christmas morning.

Let's look at a few examples here to illustrate some of the signals
and opportunities to look for to play puts for profit.

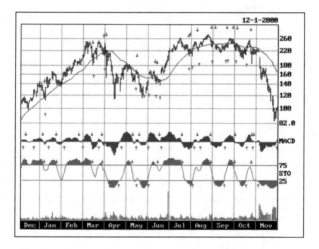

This is a chart for Broadcom (BRCM). This was one of the "dar-
lings" of Wall Street in the heat of the Internet craze, and thus,
was one of the hardest hit during the last quarter of 2000.

Notice the flattening trend from August to the end of October
when the trend started pointing down. The stock failed four
straight times to get past around $260, and on the fourth time it
quickly dropped back below the moving average. When it
approached the moving average again, the volume dried up; as
soon the price hit this point of resistance, the stock bounced
down and continued to drop dramatically for the next 30 days.

This is an example of how a stock can bounce down when it's

already in a downtrend and the stock approaches the moving average on weak volume. Notice also that the MACD formed a clear peak a couple of days prior to the dramatic drop. This was another sign of weakness that could have helped us choose a put option on this stock with confidence.

The final sign of weakness I want to point out is the breakdown through the major support level that had been established from July to the end of October at around the $220 level. Notice how dramatically the stock dropped when it finally closed below this level during the first week in November.

The at-the-money puts at the time of this downward bounce would have been the $220 puts. An investment in this put option contract would have easily produced a triple digit percentage gain over the following three weeks.

There was another example of the downward bounce from the moving average earlier in the year around the end of April and the first of May. Notice the clear peak in the MACD histogram as well as the Stochastic indicator that helped to confirm this downward bounce.

Here is SDLI, a company that is in the optical networking business. At the time of this graph, SDLI was getting ready to merge with JDSU to form an optical networking giant.

Notice the downtrend that began in August. The stock failed to rally above the moving average in September and again in October. The second move was enough to give breakout signals on the indicators, but the stock quickly lost momentum and bounced down, following the trend of the moving average. Notice the large increase in volume on the selloff.

The stock made another attempt to cross the moving average in November and failed again. Each of these failed rallies in a downtrend presented great potential for put option opportunities.

Each of the rallies that occurred after August that took the stock back close to the moving average are the kind of moves that suck many bulls back into the market. They see the breakout signals on the indicators and jump back in to buy stock or call options. As soon as the stock hits the resistance at the downtrending moving average, the rally stalls and the stock collapses again. This is what is commonly referred to as a bear trap.

If you trust indicators over trends, you'll find yourself on the wrong side of the market. If you put your emphasis on the trend, you will see these breakouts as setups to potential put plays.

To decide which put to play, I want to refer you to the rules I teach in my company's workshops on selecting call options. We try to focus on the at-the-money options and one above it and one below it. These three strike prices offer a range of choices that will fit most any forecast—from aggressive to conservative. We just apply the rule in reverse for put plays.

We look to the at-the-money put for a balance of risk and reward. We look to the in-the-money put as the more conservative; and we look to the out-of-the-money put as the more aggressive play. I like to stay with the at-the-money put if I have a high level of confidence that the stock will drop soon, and I go with the next strike in-the-money if I want to be a bit more cautious. The farther in-the-money the put, the more it costs, which may reduce your percentage return if you're right. I also like the in-the-money puts because they move closer dollar for dollar with the stock as it drops because they have a higher delta.

Delta is the term used to describe the relationship between a stock and an option. It's a value between 0-100 that tells you how much an option premium will move if the stock moves by $1. The at-the-money option typically has a delta close to 50, which means it will move approximately 50 cents for each $1 the stock moves. This can help you estimate the potential in an option play for a specific dollar move in the stock. There are also many option software programs that can help you calculate delta more precisely and project your profits based upon your forecast for the stock.

Let's look at one more example. Here is a one-year graph of Dell Computer. Dell was hit very hard in 2000 as their astronomical growth over the past five years began to show signs of slowing. This, coupled with the concerns about PC sales growth going forward, really hurt Dell. They missed ever so slightly on an earnings announcement, and since then, it's been almost straight downhill.

Let's look at this stock in more detail and talk about it a little.

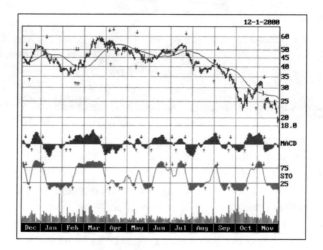

The stock was clearly in a downtrend beginning in July. However, the stock rallied to the moving average at the end of August, although it failed to stay above it, bouncing down on higher volume.

A second attempt at a breakout occurred in the middle of September, but this also failed. As we learned a moment ago, these are classic bear traps that sucked more eternally optimistic investors back into the stock because they thought it was a new breakout.

A rally in the last week of October took the stock above the moving average, but it wasn't able to sustain the climb and it quickly dropped back on very high volume. Notice again the peak in the MACD histogram and the stochastic indicator a couple of days prior to the biggest drop.

Each time the stock got close to the downtrending moving average, the volume dried up and the MACD formed a peak. All these examples represent potential opportunities for speculative put plays.

What you need to remember as you look at this example is that whenever the MACD starts to form a peak and falls off on heavier volume, you've got a potential put opportunity.

I'll say it again, "The trend is our friend." So if the trend is down, the only kind of option plays we should be considering are put plays.

We will talk about shorting stock in the next chapter for those of you who like to do that instead of playing puts. Personally, I feel much more in control with a put option than with shorting stock because I'm able to limit my risk to the premium I pay for the put.

I want to give an example of an earnings announcement put play. The stock we're going to look at for this is IBM.

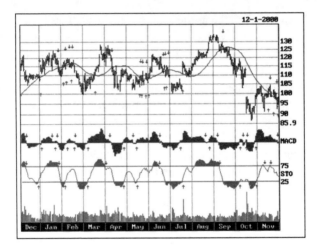

IBM peaked at an all-time high in August and quickly started to sell off. The stock crossed its short-term moving average the first week in September and continued to fall quite dramatically. I was watching this stock at the time and happened to notice that they were going to have their earnings announcement the following day. It was very clear to me that the trend of the overall market was very bearish already ... especially in the technology sector. IBM is a stock that is considered a leader in the technology sector by anybody's measure, but it was not immune to the bearish sentiment.

I determined that it would be very difficult for a company the size of IBM to come out with an earnings announcement that would surprise Wall Street enough for the stock to buck this very powerful trend. Nothing short of a miracle blowout earnings announcement could do it.

An announcement that simply met the estimates would not be enough to lift the stock above the bearish sentiment, and a miss of the estimates would surely lead to a huge sell off. In my estimation, this was a perfect earnings announcement put play. A put would be staying with the major market trend and would be tremendously profitable in the event of a steep decline in IBM shares.

I took a position in the at-the-money puts just before the close of trading and then waited after the market closed to see the announcement. I was a bit surprised that IBM actually beat the analysts' estimates by a small margin. This made me a little worried since I now had my puts. However, judging by the reaction to the announcement in after-hours trading, I knew I had a winner on my hands, making it easy to sleep that night.

When the market opened up the next day, my worries were over. The stock opened down $20, and was down even more than that at one point. I couldn't get logged onto my online trading account fast enough to take that sizable profit.

Even though IBM had beat their estimates, the stock fell in sympathy to an already downtrending market and sector. These are the kinds of trades to look for around earnings announcements in a bearish market. As is sometimes the case, when you time your put play to these pivotal news announcements, you stand a chance at a real home-run profit.

This is how to use puts for profit in a bearish market. Look for weak stocks in weak sectors or play downtrending stocks around their earnings announcements.

Let's look at some key points.

---

**Key Points**

♦ The trend is your friend

♦ Buy on weakness

♦ Sell on strength

♦ Stay close to the money

♦ 1-3 months of time

♦ Have a stop loss

♦ Sell too soon

---

The most important thing to consider before applying any investment strategy is the trend. Let me say it for the hundredth time, "The trend is your friend." The time to play puts is when the market is weak and falling. Look for sectors and industry groups where there is weakness and identify the leaders in that group.

Only play stocks that have a downtrending moving average. Don't ever try to buck the trend by picking tops in a bull market. You may miss the first opportunity when a trend changes, but if you're following closely, you'll certainly get the second opportunity and any others that follow.

When buying put options for profit, you want to buy on weakness in the market, sector, and stock. Stocks that are breaking down through areas of support or bouncing down off areas of resistance are the best prospects. One of the best signals is a downward bounce off a downtrending moving average.

Another signal that confirms weakness is peaks in the MACD

histogram. This is one of the earliest signs of weakness a stock shows. Look for other indicators to follow to confirm the breakdown before playing. As always, when in doubt, sit out.

Once you're in a put play, you want to monitor the individual stock and exit the play on the first sign of strength. An obvious sign would be a significant rise in the stock caused by some recent good news coming out on the company of the stock.

If you have identified areas of support and resistance as part of your analysis of a trade, you should consider the support area as a potential exit point. Stocks often bounce off areas of support and start new upward trends. Look for areas on the chart where the stock has bounced previously. Use these areas as exit targets.

If you follow indicators, you should consider any positive breakout as an exit signal. I like to use the MACD and watch it for positive breakouts as a signal to exit a put play. It's important to remember that ignoring a sign of strength can turn a good trade bad very quickly. One of the hardest things to do is exit a losing trade. Don't hang on to puts when the stock begins to strengthen in hopes it will weaken again and allow you to exit with a profit. There will be times when a stock begins to rise after you've bought a put and it never gives you a chance to make a profit. It's the ability to take a small loss before it becomes a big one that separates the wise put players from those who lose.

Stay close to the money when selecting your put contracts. Try to limit your selection to the at-the-money strike price—one above it or one below it. Use the price of the option to help you determine your risk. The more expensive the option, the more conservative it is. The cheaper the option, the more aggressive it is. Don't buy options just because they are cheap. The cheapest options are usually the out-of-the-money options.

I once had a wise broker tell me that if you always invest in out-of-the-money options, you'll eventually be out of money. Choose aggressive options only when you completely understand the risk and are willing to accept it.

The next key point is: one to three months of time. Most bearish moves are quick and dramatic. Thus, it makes no sense to buy options that are far from expiration when you will most likely be holding them for only a short period of time. Unless you believe the stock you're playing is headed for a long bear market, stick to contracts that are one to three months from expiration. Only choose the shortest-term options if you're certain the stock will drop by the expiration day. This may be appropriate if you're playing a potential drop on an earnings announcement that is scheduled prior to the third Friday of the current month.

I always tell my students to buy enough time, but not too much time. Remember, the longer until expiration, the more expensive the contract is. You need to balance time and cost, and the best way to do this is by selecting a contract that best fits your forecast.

You should have a stop loss on a put play just like you would for any other trade. In my experience, few options that fall in price by half of what you paid for them ever recover to the purchase price, let alone produce a profit. That's why I like to use the "50 Percent Rule" as a get-out point for any option play. If the option premium falls to half of what I paid for it, I sell it and move on. Don't take it personal. You're going to have losing trades if you play options. This just means it didn't work out to your benefit this time. It's more damaging to stay in this position and watch the equity that's left melt away as the option nears expiration than to take a loss and start looking for another good play.

The final key point: sell too soon. Perhaps you've heard the saying, "you'll never go broke taking a profit." Well it's true. Too many investors fall in love with their investments and avoid selling when they really should sell. Investments are vehicles for making money. When you've made some money, cash in and move on to the next investment.

After you go to all the work of finding a good trade, it just doesn't make any sense to hold on far after the first sign of weakness and give back all your paper profit. If you're going to be a successful investor, you need to learn how to take profits. It's always better to miss out on a little of the opportunity than to run the risk of giving back a profit. Leave a little profit on the table each time you trade and you'll find there is still plenty for you. We want to make sure we stay in good trades as long as the conditions allow and get out of the bad ones as quickly as possible; let our profits run and cut our losses short.

# Chapter Five

# Shorting Stocks

I want to briefly mention the strategy of shorting stock. Shorting stock is a strategy that's normally used by very experienced investors, to profit from declines in the stock. It's basically selling stock that you don't own, in hopes that it will drop in price so you can buy it back later at a lower price.

Selling short is basically buying low and selling high in reverse. Short sellers like to sell stock at high prices in hopes of a fall and then buy the stock to close their trade when prices are lower. Like with any trade, the profit is the difference between the buying price and the selling price, less your transaction costs.

Here's a look at the points I want to address as it relates to shorting stock.

---

### Shorting Stock

♦ Unlimited risk

♦ Sell stock you don't own in the hopes
  of buying it back later at a lower price

♦ Requires a margin deposit

♦ Buy low and sell high in reverse

♦ Always have a stop and stick to it

---

Now, let me explain what the risks are with this strategy. The risk
in short selling is substantial. You should be completely aware of
the risks if you're going to consider selling stock short.

Before you're able to short stock, you need to have a margin
account set up with your broker. Short selling is a difficult strategy for many investors to grasp because it involves selling something you don't own. You see, in the stock market, you're
allowed to sell stock you don't own as long as you buy it back
later to close out the trade.

Let me explain what's really taking place when you place an
order to sell short and perhaps this will all make a bit more sense.

I think where many investors get confused is that they think selling something you don't own is like selling something that does-
n't exist. There is a big difference. Yes, when you sell short,
you're selling stock that you don't own ... but the stock must
exist. It's not like you're dealing in fictitious shares.

If you don't own any shares and you wish to sell some shares of
a stock short, you must borrow the shares from another investor.
Don't worry; this is something your brokerage firm does for you.

You don't have to go out and find someone who owns the shares you want to sell. The broker will basically loan you the shares to sell in the market, but you need to repay the loan when you close out the trade. Closing out a short trade is called "covering." On most online trading screens the trade is entered as "buy to cover" when you exit a short sell.

I know this is a little complicated, which is part of the reason most people don't short stock ... they don't understand it. It's when you start doing trades you don't fully understand that you really get into trouble.

In order to do a short sell, you need to have, on account with your broker, margin money to prove that you have the ability to buy the shares to close the trade. Most brokers require 50 percent of the value of the stock you've shorted and then they check the price of the stock daily to make sure you still have enough money to cover the trade.

Think of the margin money as collateral for a loan. It's like putting up a good faith deposit. You can use cash or any marginable security as a margin deposit. If you have a bunch of shares of stock or even T-bills or T-bonds, you may post them as margin.

Margin requirements do vary from firm to firm. But as a rule for most stocks, you have to put up 50 percent of the value of the stock. This is typical with most firms, although there are some that will let you go a little lower. However, some may require more than 50 percent on certain stocks they have determined to be very volatile. Check with your broker to determine their specific margin requirements before considering a short sell.

Shorting stock is one of the riskiest strategies there is. In fact, the risk is theoretically unlimited. The risk you assume is anything above the price you sell the stock at. If you short a stock for $50, you then expose yourself to the risk of $1 per share that you sold for every dollar above the $50 price. As the stock rises, you are losing money. As I said earlier, you have unlimited risk because there is no limit to how high the stock can go.

This is one of those strategies where if you're really wrong, you don't just lose money, you lose your house. Your broker may come knocking on your door and take your children. (Just kidding there.) But I mean to make the important point that shorting stock can be very risky.

Let's look at how a simple short sell trade might work. Let's say you're following Yahoo! (YHOO) and that the stock is starting to show signs of weakening and the trend is starting to point down. You could use any of the signals we spoke about in the chapter on buying puts to help confirm this.

With the stock trading at $50 per share, you decide to sell short. You place an order with your broker to "sell short" 200 shares of YHOO at $50. Your account is credited with $10,000, the proceeds from the sale of 200 shares of stock at $50.

Now you monitor the stock and see that your forecast was correct. Within a week, the stock is down $10 to $40 per share. You see the stock is getting close to a level of support and you decide to exit your short position.

You place an order to "buy to cover" 200 shares of YHOO at $40, and a debit of $8,000 is made to your account. The difference between your purchase and sell is your profit. In this case, that's $2,000, less your transaction costs.

Let's look at the same example again and assume the stock moves against you. You get the credit for $10,000 when you enter the position. But this time, the stock begins to rise rather than fall. Within a week, the stock is up $10 from where you shorted it to $60. You decide to close out your position and take a loss. You place an order to "buy to cover" 200 shares at $60 and your account is debited for $12,000.

Notice you're paying more for the stock than you originally sold it for. This means you have a loss. In this case your loss is $2,000 plus the transaction costs.

If you short a stock and the stock begins to rise and you don't close out your position, you may be asked by your broker to put up more collateral or margin money. This is what's known as a margin call. I like to think of it as a call from your broker telling you you're in over your head. My advice to most is to never meet a margin call. Rather than meet the call by sending in more money, you should sell all or part of your investment to meet the margin call.

When I was in the brokerage business back in 1987, I had to make a lot of margin calls the day after "Bloody Monday." I remember going to one of the more experienced brokers that morning for a few tips on how to handle this very traumatic experience.

He said, "You simply call the customer and tell them you've got some good news and some bad news. Then tell them the good news is that one of us made money today. The bad news is it wasn't you." You see, brokers get paid to buy and to sell, whether you've made money or not.

Investors who short stock must fully understand the risk and have the financial means to weather the storm if things turn against them. It takes great personal discipline to be a good short seller. If you let emotions take control in a short sell trade, you may lose it all before you realize it.

As you can see, it is really important to have a stop loss and to stick to it. A lot of people let this run away from them. I know of people who were shorting stock during the boom in Internet stocks. They were those wise old investors who couldn't believe that a company without any earnings could possibly keep going up. Those investors were shorting stocks like Amazon, Yahoo!, DoubleClick, and many of the other Internet stocks. It didn't matter that these companies weren't making money; investors just kept pushing these stocks up and up. Many of the stocks doubled, tripled, or quadrupled in value over short periods of time.

During this time, these so-called savvy investors were shorting the stocks. They thought it would eventually be like in the *Wizard of Oz* when Toto pulled back the curtain and there was this little old man pulling the levers and pushing the buttons ... nothing like the "great and powerful Wizard" they had expected.

The problem was that these Internet stocks defied all logic and kept rising for the longest time, all the while racking up huge losses for the short sellers. Many of them met margin call after margin call, but some finally gave up and covered their short positions with substantial losses.

When the market for these stocks finally started to crumble, it was too late for many short sellers. Those who were able to weather the storm would have been richly rewarded with huge profits from the Internet stocks collapse in 2000.

When shorting stocks, it's not enough to be right, you must be right on or you could get wiped out. Hopefully, now, you can see that shorting stock is an extremely risky strategy and only for those savvy investors who have the financial means and personal discipline to manage those positions once they get into them.

When you short stock, you need to follow the market closely and be ready to take follow-up action or close out your position if the market moves against you. A sure sell signal is a reversal in the downward trend of the stock you're playing. Another exit signal is any jump in the price of the stock brought on by a surprise announcement of good news or a positive signal on the technical indicators. You can use the same 10 to 20 percent stop rule for a short position that we talked about for a normal stock position in the chapter on stop loss orders.

Hopefully, this has help you understand a little bit more about shorting stock, and has maybe answered a question or two you've had about it.

Personally, I prefer to play put options to profit from falling prices rather than shorting stock. Options have a limited risk compared to the unlimited risk of short selling. The maximum potential loss on an option purchase is the premium you paid for the option. You have total control over that because you select which put option you are going to buy.

# Chapter Six

# Collars

The final strategy I want to talk about is called a "collar," for minimizing your risk in a falling market. What's nice about this strategy is that in some cases you can still have some upside potential in the stocks you own while totally eliminating the downside.

A collar is specifically designed as a strategy for hedging a stock position. For those of you who actually own stocks right now, this strategy is something you should definitely take a closer look at.

A collar is an easy way to get stock insurance. In a minute I'm going to show you how to get someone else to pay for that insurance. In a sense, this is like getting a free insurance policy on stock you own.

## Collars - Free Insurance

♦ Use on stocks you own

♦ Sell covered calls

♦ Use income to buy puts

♦ Insures against losses

♦ Depending on stock, may still allow for upside potential

The foundation of the collar strategy is stock you already own that you want to protect in a bear market. The basic concept of a collar involves combining two simple conservative option strategies, first a covered call and second a protective put.

In case you're not familiar with the covered call strategy, let's take just a minute to cover the basic concepts of one. If you own stock, you have the right to give another investor the opportunity to buy it from you. One way to do this is by selling a call option. Once again, we're going to be selling something we do not own, just like selling stock short.

When you sell an option, you accept an obligation. In the case of a call option, the obligation is to sell 100 shares of the underlying stock at the strike price for each contract you sell. If you already own the stock to fulfill this potential obligation, this trade is "covered." If you do not own the stock to fulfill the potential obligation to sell stock at the strike price, the trade is said to be "naked."

Covered calls are one of the most conservative option strategies. It's an option strategy that most brokers will permit in a retirement account. A naked call, on the other hand, is one of the riskiest option strategies. Like selling stock short, the risk of a naked call is unlimited. You basically give someone the right to buy stock from you at a set price on or before the expiration day of the option. If the stock rises above the strike price of that option, you are obligated to buy stock at the current higher price to fulfill your obligation. Since there is no limit on how high a stock may rise, the naked call has virtually unlimited risk.

When you sell a call option, you collect a premium from the buyer, although you'll never actually meet the buyer of the call options you sell. The options exchange and your brokerage firm handle the process of matching option buyers and sellers. You never have to worry about finding a buyer if you want to sell call options. You simply need to check the current bid price being offered for the call contract you want to sell and then place an order. The exchange will match your order with a buyer willing to pay you the market price for the call. The income from the call option sell is deposited into your account the next business day. It's worth mentioning that option trades settle in one day whereas stock trades normally take three days to settle.

When you sell a covered call, you are basically giving another investor the opportunity to buy your stock at the strike price of the call option on or before expiration day. They will normally only exercise their right to buy your stock if the price on expiration day is higher than the strike price of the call option you sold. This would basically mean that they are buying stock from you at a below market price. When they do this, it is referred to as being "called out."

Your broker will automatically sell your stock at the strike price of your call and leave the proceeds in your account. It's possible to avoid being called out by buying back the call option prior to expiration day. If the stock has risen since you sold the call, there is a chance you will have to pay a higher price to buy it back than the premium you collected when you sold it. In this case you would suffer a loss on the option transaction. However, keep in mind that if the stock has risen, the value of the shares you own will have also gone up. The rise in the value of your stock will usually offset most or all of the loss from buying back the call option. Keep this in mind as we explain the collar because it's an easy way to get out of the obligation to sell your stock if you decide to remove the collar before expiration day.

As I mentioned before, the second part of a collar is a protective put. This is the insurance aspect of the collar strategy that provides the downside protection against a decline in the price of the stock you own.

The collar strategy can virtually eliminate the risk of owning stock. You can apply the collar strategy to any optionable stock in your portfolio and know that even a fall to zero would not wipe you out. It's a very comforting feeling if the market has you worried. You can apply a collar and go on vacation knowing your portfolio will be in tact when you return. And to think that you can set up this strategy without risking any of your own money makes it all the better. Let's take a closer look.

The first step in applying the collar strategy is to determine which of the stocks that you own might need a collar. Any stocks that have you worried could be due for a correction or stocks that could be sucked down by a downturn in the market should be considered candidates. Stocks that are uptrending are not good candidates for collars. Applying a collar to an uptrending stock could result in being called out of the stock, and it might cause you to miss a significant upward move. So the collar should be considered a defensive strategy that is used to preserve your equity in bearish market conditions. It is not a strategy that will result in windfall profits, but rather one that will help to avoid catastrophic losses caused by unexpected drops in the market.

Once you determine a stock you wish to protect, you first sell one call option for each 100 shares you own. This is the covered call strategy we mentioned a moment ago. The strike price you select is normally either the at-the-money contract or the one above it. You want to allow yourself a little margin for error if the stock should rise rather than fall. By selecting a call option for your covered call that has a strike price slightly higher than the current price of the stock, you give yourself a little upside potential. Do not sell more call options than you have shares to cover. Remember, 100 shares per contract.

The income you collect from the covered calls is what you are going to use to purchase some protective puts. Then, select your protective puts using the same criteria we spoke about earlier in the chapter on buying puts. Normally you'll buy either the at-the-money contract or the next one down. This is the basic mechanics of the collar trade. I like to think of a collar as the free insurance strategy.

Let's look at an example using Cisco stock to see how a collar works.

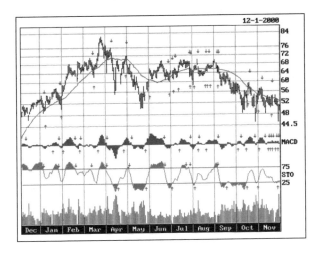

Here is a graph of Cisco Systems for a one-year period. Looking at the far right side of the graph, you can see that the stock has been in a downtrend since the end of August and has been consolidating in the $48-54 range. Based on the fact that the stock has traded in this range two times prior to this occurrence and moved higher, this range would be considered the stock support.

In order to consider a collar at this time, you need to consider the upside for CSCO to be somewhat limited in the short term. You also have to be concerned about a drop below the established support level in the $48 range. If that is your analysis, this is a perfect time to look at using a collar or a hedge.

Let's say you want to go on a vacation for two or three months and when you return, you want to make sure your portfolio is still intact. This is another good reason to consider applying the collar strategy. This is how it might work.

Here is the call option quotes table for the April 2001 options that are five months out from the present month.

| Apr 21, 2001 Call Series - CSCO $50.625 | | | | | | |
|---|---|---|---|---|---|---|
| Symbol | Issue | Intrinsic Value | Bid | Asked | Volume | Open Interest |
| CYQ DG | CSCO APR 21, 2001 $ 35.000 CALL | 15.625 | 18.625 | 19.125 | 0 | 397 |
| CWY DI | CSCO APR 21, 2001 $ 45.000 CALL | 5.625 | 11.750 | 12.250 | 11 | 910 |
| CWY DJ | CSCO APR 21, 2001 $ 50.000 CALL | 0.625 | 9.000 | 9.500 | 42 | 8204 |
| CWY DK | CSCO APR 21, 2001 $ 55.000 CALL | | 6.500 | 6.875 | 14 | 8667 |
| CWY DL | CSCO APR 21, 2001 $ 60.000 CALL | | 4.625 | 4.875 | 25 | 9224 |
| CWY DM | CSCO APR 21, 2001 $ 65.000 CALL | | 3.250 | 3.625 | 112 | 12282 |
| CWY DN | CSCO APR 21, 2001 $ 70.000 CALL | | 2.312 | 2.500 | 10 | 14285 |
| CWY DO | CSCO APR 21, 2001 $ 75.000 CALL | | 1.375 | 1.625 | 12 | 8031 |
| CWY DP | CSCO APR 21, 2001 $ 80.000 CALL | | 0.875 | 1.062 | 15 | 9460 |

*12/01/00 - 10:59 a.m. Eastern. Current Stock Quotes are delayed a minimum of 20 minutes*

Considering the forecast for CSCO is limited on the upside, you want to focus on the contracts that are near and slightly above the current price of the stock, which is $50.525. This leads you to the $50 and $55 contracts. Since you are slightly optimistic on the stock, you want to give yourself a little upside potential if the stock should rally between now and April. Choosing the April 55 call option gives you almost $5 of upside potential before you put yourself in jeopardy of being called out of your stock. You collect a premium of $650 for each call option you sell.

Options are generally quoted in "per share" increments. To figure out the cost or income for one contract, multiply the quote by 100 because there are 100 shares in each option contract. You then sell one call option for each 100 shares of CSCO stock you own.

Now you've constructed the first half of the collar. The second half is constructed by purchasing protective puts. Here is an option quote table for the April 2001 puts on CSCO. We chose the same expiration month for the puts as we used for the calls to simplify the trade and to make it easier to manage.

| Apr 21, 2001 Put Series - CSCO $50.875 | | | | | | |
|---|---|---|---|---|---|---|
| Symbol | Issue | Intrinsic Value | Bid | Asked | Volume | Open Interest |
| CYQ PG | CSCO APR 21, 2001 $ 35.000 PUT | | 2.187 | 2.437 | 1 | 913 |
| CWY PI | CSCO APR 21, 2001 $ 45.000 PUT | | 5.000 | 5.375 | 20 | 7295 |
| CWY PJ | CSCO APR 21, 2001 $ 50.000 PUT | | 7.125 | 7.500 | 92 | 23366 |
| CWY PK | CSCO APR 21, 2001 $ 55.000 PUT | 4.125 | 9.500 | 10.000 | 10 | 7507 |
| CWY PL | CSCO APR 21, 2001 $ 60.000 PUT | 9.125 | 12.500 | 13.125 | 15 | 4940 |
| CWY PM | CSCO APR 21, 2001 $ 65.000 PUT | 14.125 | 16.125 | 16.750 | 0 | 1819 |
| CWY PN | CSCO APR 21, 2001 $ 70.000 PUT | 19.125 | 20.000 | 20.625 | 0 | 1338 |
| CWY PO | CSCO APR 21, 2001 $ 75.000 PUT | 24.125 | 24.250 | 25.125 | 0 | 438 |
| CWY PP | CSCO APR 21, 2001 $ 80.000 PUT | 29.125 | 28.750 | 29.750 | 0 | 275 |

*12/01/00 - 11:00 a.m. Eastern. Current Stock Quotes are delayed a minimum of 20 minutes*

After having determined that the support for the stock is in the $48 area, you want to look for a put that will protect you against a decline in the stock beyond that point. The nearest strike price is the $45 put. You can purchase one contract of the $45 put for $537.50.

Notice that the income you collect from selling the $55 call is $650 and the cost of the $45 put is just $537.50. This means you are able to cover the entire cost of the protective put from the proceeds of the covered call and still have a credit to your account of more than $100 for each 100 shares you place in the collar. If you have 500 shares of CSCO, sell five call contracts and buy five put contracts to create the collar. This gives you about $5 of upside potential in the event of a rally, but protect you against any decline in the price of the stock beyond $45. Plus, you collect $100 of excess income from the collar to minimize your downside even more.

Looking back at our option quote tables, you could also construct a collar using the $50 put and call. You could collect $900 per contract from the sell of the $50 call and pay $750 to buy the $50 put. This totally limits your upside potential, but protects you completely against any decline in the stock. You can see that the range of option contracts available offers tremendous flexibility to construct a collar for almost any possible forecast you might have.

With the collar in place, we are now hedged. We can take our vacation and know that when we return, our portfolio will be intact no matter what the stock does while we're away. We don't even need to monitor the position until we return because we know we're protected. In the first example, our maximum loss—even had CSCO dropped to zero—would be around $4 per share.

On the upside, we have given ourselves $5 of an upside move before we would ever get called out. Although we have capped our upside potential by selling a covered call, we have still given ourselves room to make some additional money if the stock rises.

This is a wonderful strategy that every investor should understand. It really is free stock insurance. Just imagine how different you might feel right now had you used the collar strategy to protect yourself against the potential of a bear market when stocks began to turn south in March of 2000. You could have preserved your portfolio profits at the peak of the market and it wouldn't have cost you a dime to do it.

Now when you are too scared to stay in the market, but you don't want to sell everything, which triggers tax consequences, why not apply a simple collar? This is a great a way to protect you portfolio while you are waiting out a bear market.

So let's review our Cisco Systems collar example:

---

### Cisco Systems Collar

♦ Stock currently at $50

♦ Put protects you from a loss below $45

♦ Income from calls pays for puts

♦ Allows upside to $55

---

With the stock trading at just above $50, we sell the $55 call and collect some income. This gives us a bit of upside potential before being put at risk of getting called out of our stock. Then, we use the income from the call options to buy the $45 put. The put will protect us against any decline in the stock beyond $45. The difference between $45 and $50 is our deductible, or in other words, the risk we are willing to incur on the downside. After we pay for the puts, we still have $1 left over, which reduces our total downside risk to about $4 per share.

Now let's look at how to close out a collar as expiration day nears or when we see the stock begin to form a new uptrend. Closing it out can be done anytime before the option expires—in this case, anytime before the third Friday in April. When you remove a collar, you're basically "uncovering" your stock and closing out your insurance policy.

---

## Closing Out a Collar

♦ Can be closed anytime before expiration

♦ Sell puts and buy back calls

♦ Stock goes up – let stock get called

♦ Stock goes down – sell puts keep stock

♦ Stock stays the same – free insurance

---

To get out of one of these trades, we simply just do the opposite of what we did to get into it. Remember, we sold calls and we bought puts. So to get out of the collar, we're going to buy calls and/or sell puts.

Buying back our covered calls uncovers our stock and removes the potential of getting called out of it. We must do this prior to expiration day if we don't want to run the risk of having our stock called away. Then, we sell the put options for whatever value there is and collect some money. The value of the puts will likely be very small, unless the stock has dropped since you applied the collar, so make sure you can at least collect enough to cover the cost of the commission for selling them or simply let them expire; it's not a big deal. It's just like the insurance company getting to keep your homeowner's premium because your house didn't burn down.

That's the general concept of closing out a collar. Now let's look at the specifics based on what the stock does after you apply the collar. There are basically three things that can happen after you apply the collar: the stock can go up, down, or sideways. Let's look at each and explain how you might react.

If the stock rises after you create your collar, you may need to take some follow-up action based upon your forecast for the stock going forward. If the stock has risen above the strike price of your covered call, you are in jeopardy of getting called out of your shares. You need to determine if that's what you want or if you'd rather get out of this situation so you can keep your shares.

I'm usually one to say that if you're going to get called out, let the shares go. Too often I've seen investors buy back the call options to avoid getting called out only to have the stock drop once they no longer have the protection the call offered. I consider getting called out to be too much of a good thing, not a bad thing.

Much like with a traditional covered call play, you've got two forces at work on the premium of the call. The natural decay of time is reducing the value of the call while the rise in the stock is increasing it. If the stock rises substantially over the strike price of the covered call, you may be faced with the prospect of paying more to buy the call back than you collected when you sold it. This creates a loss, but you should remember that the shares of stock you own will have risen dollar for dollar with the stock and should create enough of an increase in your equity to offset the loss. It's when I'm going to take a large loss by buying back the call that I usually choose to simply let my shares get called away. With trading costs at such reasonable levels, I can always re-enter the stock position if I decide I still want to own it ... and all it will cost me is another commission.

If the stock has risen, but not passed the strike price of the covered call, you do not have to worry about getting called out. The call option will expire worthless and you'll be in a position to decide whether you want to place another collar for the next month or perhaps just a covered call ... or perhaps leave your stock uncovered completely. The choice is yours.

If the stock declines after you place a collar, it will reduce or eliminate your risk. If the stock falls and remains below the strike price of the call, the call option will usually expire worthless. The put, on the other hand, will increase in value as the stock price falls. If you selected a put with a strike price below the price of the stock, you will have to wait until you cover your deductible before the benefits of the protective put kick in. Once the stock passes the strike price of your protective put, you're insured dollar for dollar all the way to zero.

On or before expiration day, you need to decide if you'd like to exercise your put or simply sell it. Exercising the put results in your stock being sold at the strike price. If the stock has fallen since you put on the collar, this will most likely be an above market price, and you might be very happy to sell your shares at that price and move on.

The most common thing investors in this position do is simply sell the put option and use the profit to offset the paper loss on their stock. This allows them to keep their stock and not realize any gain or loss on a sale for tax purposes.

The final scenario is if the stock doesn't go down or up, but stays right where it was when you put on the collar. In this scenario, you don't need to anything. The covered calls can expire worthless as can the protective puts. You have had the benefit of the insurance without any cost and now you're in a position to decide what you want to do with your stock going forward.

If you still like the stock and feel the company has potential, you can choose to hold on to your shares. But if you no longer believe this company has promise, you are free to sell and move on. You are also in a position to apply the collar or any other strategy that allows you to extend the trade with some form of insurance or income. It's nice to have options! (Pun intended!)

The collar is a wonderful strategy. It is simple, effective, and easy to monitor. You can put a collar on for two or three months—or however long you are worried about the market— and almost forget about it. I find a collar makes me almost wish my stock would fall so I could get the satisfaction of knowing I picked the right strategy to protect my investment. Imagine wishing your stocks would fall...

Let's look at some key points to summarize the collar strategy.

---

## Key Points

♦ Sell enough calls to pay for puts

♦ Use out-of-the-money options

♦ Use two or three-month options

♦ It is easiest to use options that expire at the same time

---

Make sure you sell enough call options to generate the cash necessary to pay for the puts. As you check the option quotes on stocks you own, you may find there are some that allow a little flexibility in how many calls you must sell to pay for the puts. The key is to make sure you're totally covered on the downside for all the shares you own. If you don't cover all your shares, it's not a problem ... it could actually be a big benefit. By not covering all your shares, you have some that are not at risk of getting called away no matter how high the stock may go. Leaving some shares uncovered allows you to have a greater upside potential on your collar. So try to sell just enough calls to pay for the puts you need to buy. Look at the protective puts you plan to buy and then figure out exactly how many calls you need to sell in order to cover their cost.

Let's say you have 1,000 shares and you decide you want to buy the protective put with the first strike below the current price of the stock. Let's assume for this example that this put is trading for $3. To purchase 10 contracts to protect your 1,000 shares will cost you $3,000. Let's say that when you look at the call options, you see that you can sell the first contract above the price of the stock and collect a premium of $5. It will only take six contracts of the call options to generate the $3,000 you need to cover the cost of the protective puts. You could sell six covered calls and leave 400 of your shares uncovered. This would allow you to profit on those 400 shares by as much as the stock happens to rise without worrying that your stock might be called away.

I like to set up my collars using out-of-the-money options. This means that I prefer to look at the call options with strike prices just above the current stock price and put options just below it. By going out-of-the-money, you'll find the options are cheaper and make it easier to get the benefits the collar provides.

It is easiest to use options that expire at the same time when you do a collar. There is no rule that says it only works if the options expire at the same time, but it will complicate your collar if the put and call expire at different times.

Let's say you don't feel like you want to have your stock covered for more than a month, but you want the downside protection for two months. You could sell a call that is out just one month and buy a put that is out two. The problem with this is that it will make the options difficult to match in price. You may find that the money you collect from covering 100 percent of your shares is not enough to cover the puts you want to buy. In some circumstances that might be fine, but it does make the collar a bit more difficult to create and you may lose the added benefit of doing it without any out-of-pocket expense.

I firmly believe that every investor should learn the collar strategy if they are going to invest in a volatile market. When the market gets choppy, the collar provides an easy way to move to the sidelines and to sit things out without selling out.

Simply put, a collar a low-risk strategy that allows you to make a mistake and still not get hurt too bad. That makes the collar a good strategy to use to learn more about how options work. I hope you enjoy this new arrow in your quiver.

# Summary

As we bring things to a conclusion I want to make sure you understand that investing in a volatile or bear market doesn't have to be hard, it's just different. If you understand the simple ways to protect yourself against losses and find opportunity as stocks fall, you'll be a better investor.

Markets don't always go up, but most investors seem to expect them to. When stocks begin to fall, many investors simply don't know what to do. As a result, they continue to do what they have found to be successful in a bull market, but with dramatically different results.

When you're prepared for anything and have the tools to adapt your investing to a change in the market, the impact can be dramatic. The one or two percent you save by using a stop or a protective put could amount to thousands of more dollars in your account by the time you get to retirement age. That's the value of a financial education.

I thought it might be wise to summarize some of the important points I've tried to make throughout the course of this book so that you have a good idea of where to start. The worst thing you can do at this point is nothing. So try to find one thing you've read in this book that can have a positive impact on your investing and start there. Continue to experiment and test the other strategies until you find the ones that work for you.

## Summary

♦ Don't let your emotions take over

♦ The trend is your friend

♦ Cash is king

♦ Live to trade another day

Hopefully, you feel more confident about investing now that you have some tools and resources to help you in a down market or a volatile market. When the market is bearish, you need to do two things; the first is to protect your portfolio from losing money and the second is to find ways to profit when stocks are falling.

There is always someone making money in the stock market, no matter what the market is doing. There is always an opportunity if you know where to look and how to take advantage of it. Hopefully you've picked up on a few ways now as we've gone through this *Bear Market Game Plan, Strategies for Investing in a Volatile Market*.

There are just a few things I want you to keep in mind. The best thing you can do now, after having read this book, is to go through each of the examples again. I have detailed them very clearly here, and hopefully you can look at these and follow along. Get online and start looking at some of the stocks you own or the stocks you have been watching. Apply some of the things we've talked about and see if you can put yourself in the mindset and apply the things we have discussed in order to feel confident with them. Knowledge helps make you more confident in the decisions you make when your money is at stake.

The first thing we have to learn is to control our emotions, especially the emotion of fear—the fear of losing money, the fear of making a mistake, or the fear of admitting we have made a mistake. There is also the more subtle fear of not wanting to give up a profit. All of these fears are important to know and recognize. Failure to recognize them when your emotions are impacting your investment decisions can lead to significant losses.

You should try to overcome the tendency to be an eternal optimist. The eternal optimist is usually the last one out of the market after everyone else has already run for the exit. It's not a very pleasant position to be in. Some of you might feel like you're in that spot right now. It's vitally important for you to understand that the markets don't always go up. We have been spoiled rotten over the last few years because they have. But we've gotten a little dose of reality lately as the markets turned bearish. Take heart; this, too, shall pass.

The next thing is to recognize that the trend is your friend. I think recognizing trends is one of the most important skills you need to acquire as an investor. I've emphasized this throughout and given you some approaches, strategies, and resources to help you recognize the trends. Before you ever invest a penny, you should be aware of the major trends in the market, sectors, and individual stocks you are considering putting your money in. When the trend is moving up, that's when you want to be invested.

Never trust technical indicators over trends. They should be used in conjunction to help you make important investment decisions. Trusting indicators more than trends may result in getting caught in those bear traps we spoke about. So stick with the indicators in the uptrending markets and you will find a higher percentage of success in your trades.

A bull market has followed nearly every bear market in the history of the stock market. After the last major bear market in 1974, the market rose for six straight years and eight of the next nine. The total rise in the market over that period of time was a staggering 366%.

Fortunately, bear markets are usually over quickly and we get back to investing on the upside of the market. The key is to make

sure you have some money left to invest when the market finally turns. That's why I like to say "cash is king" in a bear market.
If you blow out your account in the bear market, you won't have
any capital left to invest when the bargains are abundant and the
market starts to rise again.

At the beginning of this book I asked you to ask yourself if you
would be better off today had you earned interest on your money
over the last half of 2000 rather than having it invested in your
portfolio? All of a sudden interest isn't looking like the same old
boring investment you thought it was. There is a time to be
aggressive and there are times to be conservative. The key is recognizing the difference.

The last thing is the most important. The number one rule of
investing should always be "live to trade another day." I don't
mean that literally, but figuratively. We don't want to risk everything we have on one bad trade. A mistake like that would make
it impossible to ever recover. Money management and risk management are critical elements of any successful investing program. This really holds true when it comes to investing in a bear
market. Don't be an eternal optimist riding a bad trade down to
nothing. There are plenty of signals ... plenty of warning signs
telling you to get out before that point.

As I look back on my individual investing experience, I see that
I've learned this valuable lesson. I can remember times when it
was easy to risk all my savings on one single trade in hopes of a
big windfall profit. (It seems like we all like to take the biggest
risks with our money when we can least afford the consequences.) Now that I'm in a position to take substantial risks and
live with the consequences, I can't bring myself to the point to
take them anymore. Experience is a great teacher.

I believe that a wise man learns from his mistakes, but a wiser
man learns from the mistakes of others. I've made many mistakes with my own money and investments. I hope you're able to
learn from some of the lessons I've learned so you can avoid the
consequences of making bad decisions. If you can avoid one bad

trade after reading this book, you'll have gotten a great return on your investment of time and money spent to get it.

So there you have it, a few simple tools to help you manage your investments in a volatile market. Now you can honestly say you have a "Bear Market Game Plan" to help you survive in this challenging market. As bleak as this may get, let me assure you that there will be another nice bull market again (hopefully sooner rather than later). It will be another great opportunity to play the upside of the market. Remember there are always corrections along the way in the stock market. Success comes through learning now how to adjust your positions and approaches as well as handling the emotions that will always be present.

Thanks for reading. I hope it has been a great experience for you. I hope I'll have the opportunity to help you learn more about investing in one of my company's many investing seminars and workshops. I've included some additional information about our various training programs in the back of this book.

More information is also available online at our web site, www.investortoolbox.com.

Best of luck, and we'll see you online.

# If you enjoy this book...

...you'll love the other products produced and presented by Ross Jardine and his associates. Each course is designed to help you with your personal investments in the stock market.

◆ **The Bear Market Game Plan Manual & Video Instructional Course**

With the stock market as volatile as it's ever been, people are losing money. Learn how to protect your portfolio in a bear market, and even take advantage of it for profit!

◆ **Attend an Online Investors Advantage Two-Day Instructional Workshop**

No one cares more about your money than you do. This workshop teaches you how to take control of your own investments in order to grow your portfolio.

◆ **Attend Steve Wirrick's Advanced Options Strategies Two-Day Workshop**

For the seasoned investor, this two-day workshop goes through the various strategies options offer in varying market conditions, showing you how to create monthly cash flow using your investments.

◆ **The Advanced Options Strategies Manual & Video Homestudy Course**

This homestudy course takes those investors who are ready to trade options through the Advanced Options Strategies course at home and at their own pace.

**For more information on these products or services, call 1-800-393-5123.**